The Year of Learning Dangerously

The Year of Learning Dangerously

Adventures in Homeschooling

* * *

Quinn Cummings

A PERIGEE BOOK

A PERIGEE BOOK
Published by the Penguin Group
Penguin Group (USA) Inc.
375 Hudson Street, New York, New York 10014, USA

Penguin Group (Canada), 90 Eglinton Avenue East, Suite 700, Toronto, Ontario M4P 2Y3, Canada (a division of Pearson Penguin Canada Inc.) • Penguin Books Ltd., 80 Strand, London WC2R 0RL, England • Penguin Group Ireland, 25 St. Stephen's Green, Dublin 2, Ireland (a division of Penguin Books Ltd.) • Penguin Group (Australia), 250 Camberwell Road, Camberwell, Victoria 3124, Australia (a division of Pearson Australia Group Pty. Ltd.) • Penguin Books India Pvt. Ltd., 11 Community Centre, Panchsheel Park, New Delhi—110 017, India • Penguin Group (NZ), 67 Apollo Drive, Rosedale, Auckland 0632, New Zealand (a division of Pearson New Zealand Ltd.) • Penguin Books (South Africa) (Pty.) Ltd., 24 Sturdee Avenue, Rosebank, Johannesburg 2196, South Africa

Penguin Books Ltd., Registered Offices: 80 Strand, London WC2R 0RL, England

Text design by Tiffany Estreicher

First edition: August 2012

Library of Congress Cataloging-in-Publication Data

Cummings, Quinn.
The year of learning dangerously : adventures in homeschooling / Quinn Cummings.—First edition.
pages cm. (A Perigee book)
ISBN 978-0-399-53760-8
1. Home schooling—United States. 2. Cummings, Quinn—Anecdotes. I. Title.
LC40.C66 2012
371.04'20973—dc23 2012014182

PRINTED IN THE UNITED STATES OF AMERICA
10 9 8 7 6 5 4 3 2 1

This book is dedicated to my daughter

Midway upon the journey of our life
I found myself within a forest dark,
For the straightforward pathway had been lost.

—Dante Alighieri

When you come to a fork in the road, take it.

—Yogi Berra

Contents

Breathless

* * *

I was hiding in the laundry room fighting off a full-blown panic attack. If long division with remainders hadn't been invented, this would not have been happening.

Actually, panic attack isn't the correct diagnosis. A panic attack is typically a response to an imaginary threat, but there was nothing imaginary at work here. I had a rock-solid reason to be slumped on the linoleum wheezing into a paper bag. I had been homeschooling my daughter for two whole days and found myself suddenly, brutally aware of how completely unqualified I was for this assignment. Here was my child—my one shot at creating a decent, kind, productive member of society—and I was treating her like a goldfish I'd won at a carnival.

I was entirely incompetent to educate my own offspring. Sitting there in my miserable, hyperventilating state, I remembered that I'd spent weeks and weeks trying to teach Alice how to tie her shoes. Then, one afternoon at a playdate, a four-year-old friend taught her how to do it perfectly. I was less qualified to educate my child than someone who had to be reminded not to lick the class guinea pig. Perhaps I should find a preschooler to replace me for the next eight years, someone to educate my daughter while I live quietly here in the laundry room, folding underwear and otherwise not doing my child harm. I breathed slowly and carefully into the paper bag and tried to remember why I was doing this.

School. Daze.

* * *

In the beginning, much of education came easily to Alice, as it had come to me. I'm not saying we're smarter than the average bear; I've know quite a few people with lovely large brains for whom school was a years-long exercise in frustration and humiliation. No, the key to this easiness was reading. My family seems to be wired for literacy. I started reading at an early age and because reading was fun and stories were excellent, I read a great deal. This, predictably, made me a better reader. By the time I started nursery school, anything having to do with letters fell upon me as gentle rain that I soaked up with delight. Eventually this led to my skipping second grade, which turned out to be the last time I over-achieved in a classroom. Academic apathy aside, I never lost my enthusiasm for reading, and in the fullness of time I had a wonderful daughter to whom I read constantly. I read to her because I loved reading, because it provided a great opportunity to snuggle with my kid and because I hated playing Candy Land.

It came to pass that Alice, too, read on her own before she set foot in a formal classroom. Because she could read, her preschool teacher suggested Alice skip kindergarten. I suspect a less neurotic person might have been proud of her child for skipping, or pleased at the opportunities academic acceleration might provide. I, on the other hand, became miserably convinced that letting her skip a grade meant I had just shortened her childhood by one year. I spent much of the rest of the school year humming "Cat's in the Cradle" and "Sunrise, Sunset," patting Alice's head dolefully while noting how very tiny she was and fixating on life's terrible brevity. One night, I had to be restrained from waking Alice to extract a promise that she wouldn't attend college out of state. My psychic hand-wringing notwithstanding, skipping a grade seemed to be the right choice. Alice sailed through first grade, approaching anything in print the way a killer whale would attack a wounded seal. We word-people aren't playing when it comes to books.

Sadly, the universe isn't made up of only letters and words. I didn't like numbers as a kid, I don't like numbers now and my kid doesn't like numbers that much, either. Maybe there's a connection. We prefer intellectual pursuits that have the potential for nuance and subtlety, that allow for inspiration and poetry and that reward spontaneous invention when one isn't paying close attention to a teacher's question at that critical moment. Numbers sneer at the digressive rejoinder. Numbers scorn the literary allusion. Numbers have all the spontaneity of a tank parade through Red Square.

"Quinn, what is seven times eight?"

"Well, it's probably less than nine times eight and it might be sixty-something and it's certainly not a hair ribbon."

That's not me in elementary school. That's me now. When Alice reached second grade, she started to gripe about multiplication. I patted her shoulder with genuine sympathy and put my treasured *Schoolhouse Rock!* tape on a repeating loop. Within a few weeks, both of us were pretty certain that seven times eight was fifty-six, but then came division. Division never made it to *Schoolhouse Rock!* so we had no mnemonic ditties to help us through. More than a few tears were shed, but eventually—with the help of a persistent teacher and a haranguing mother—Alice managed to wrestle simple division to the mat. We all rejoiced.

Third grade brought a couple of weeks of refresher arithmetic before long division started showing up in the homework packet. Whatever distaste Alice felt for addition, subtraction and multiplication was dwarfed by her loathing of long division and its hellish spawn, remainders. She took remainders personally. Had the division just tried a little harder, she felt, there wouldn't be these sulfurous minions left hanging out there, taunting and offending all humanity. Alice decided not to reward long division's bad behavior by actually learning it, choosing instead the elementary school version of a sit-down strike. For one entire school year, she insisted she couldn't possibly master long division; it was eternally beyond her ability, so she'd simply ignore it.

I explained in increasingly unladylike tones that if she made even a modest effort to decipher its mysteries now, long division would go away forever. But that's not how she saw it. To Alice's way of thinking—and history had thus far proven her right—once she did crack long division, they'd only throw something more unpleasant at her. No, her best strategy would be to engage this known enemy in a siege.

Her third-grade teacher was wonderful and dimpled, young and enthusiastic. I was none of these things, but together we guided Alice toward mastery of long division with its oily, devilish remainders by the following spring. I can't point to a single other thing she learned that year, but it didn't matter. By May, we had moved long division into the "done" column, remainders and all. Now, I could start nagging about more traditionally maternal concerns like flossing and sun protection.

When September rolled around, as it tends to do that time of year, Alice began the fourth grade. At the end of the first week, I flipped open her shiny new backpack and discovered page after page of long division problems. Even my innumerate brain could see these nasty buggers were going to have remainders. I fanned the worksheets in her direction.

"Why are these back?"

She glanced up for a second, then went back to the Roald Dahl book she was reading. I waved my hand between her eyes and the page she was reading, a page filled with gloriously obedient words—not a number among them.

"Why," I asked slowly, "am I looking at long division with remainders . . . again?"

"We did some problems this week and I didn't know how to do them. The teacher says I need to learn it."

Because it had worked so well the year before, Alice convinced her teacher she couldn't do long division with remainders and was quite prepared to spend the next eight months pretending to learn something she already knew quite well. On more than several occasions I explained to Alice's fourth-grade teacher that he was being gamed. On more than several occasions his response was the same: *Do you mean to imply that this petite, doe-eyed creature—a sweet-natured girl who is reduced to helpless tears by this arbitrary and alien math concept—is pulling a fast one on me, a seasoned professional? Oh, I don't think so.*

Of course, by now I had observed her zoom through a page of long division problems in under three minutes when promised a bribe-Barbie—so I had a slightly more jaundiced view of her abilities, both arithmetic and histrionic. Quite miraculously, Alice reconquered long division with remainders during her last week of fourth grade. She was fond of her teacher, and I suspect this was her year-end gift to him.

Her reading and mathematics levels were now several car lengths' apart, and reading had the turbo under its hood. Daniel and I decided to move her from the sweet supportive school with the lovely teachers to the French-immersion school with the frowning teachers. My hope was that learning French full-time would give her brain something to do and that mathematics might be more captivating if it were spelled *mathématiques*. Hey, it worked for Perrier.

Two weeks before fifth grade was to start, on a warm, lazy August afternoon, I ran Alice through a page of long division problems. She sighed and fussed and carried on a bit, but she finished them perfectly. The new school promised to be more challenging, and I looked forward to nagging my daughter at a new level of intensity. The second week of school, I was paging through her homework packet and suddenly recoiled in horror. I would have been less taken aback discovering a swamp adder coiled around her pencil case. In a cold, anxious voice I asked, "Why is there long division with remainders in here?"

"Because," she said distractedly, reading *The Lightning Thief* while perfecting her headstand on the couch. "The teacher gave—"

"Let me guess," I cut her off. "They tested you last week and you didn't do any of the long division with remainders, because you're *you*. So now they think you don't know how to do them."

"Um," she said vaguely, but her brain was already off this tiresome subject and back to the place where people her age do fierce battle with genuine evil, not leftover digits.

In that instant, I saw her academic future, and it looked terribly familiar. Everything that came easily to me, I did. Anything that required actual work caused me to become the academic equivalent of an opossum feigning death, including foul emanations and facial rictus. I never actually learned how to learn—which is, after all, the ultimate goal of primary education. An adult is rarely confronted with a pop quiz on Ponce de León, but every time an adult faces a new challenge, he either put his shoulder into it or he runs away. I still have this nagging feeling I'm supposed to *know* stuff without actually *learning* it, and that anything requiring a mental effort beyond snatching the answer from memory simply proves I was never that smart to begin with. Alice's classroom instructors had all been very good teachers and well intentioned, but when it came to willpower and sheer animal cunning, she was the master. I started to fear that the hidden lesson she was taking away from her classroom experiences was, *There's no need to exert yourself. Just let the academic tide passively carry you along.* In a few decades she'd be just like her mother, wondering how much she could have accomplished had she actually learned to swim.

By midway through the year, we knew the new school wasn't going to work. The English was even more rudimentary than in the previous school, which made sense when I realized half the school were French speakers trying to learn English. It might have been nice had I thought of that in August, before I wrote the check. Alice was coasting through anything to do with letters and feigning brain trauma when it came to anything to do with numbers. Our options were limited.

We could stay at this school and hope for a brilliant teacher with experience in labor negotiation or a sudden change in Alice's attitude, neither of which was likely. Or we could look for another school. This is what my mother tried over and over again when I was a child, only to discover that I could underachieve in three different area codes. Something told me we'd try school after school and Alice would cry tear after arithmetic-hating tear, and arrange to be the first person to ever graduate from high school without finishing elementary school math.

Or we could homeschool Alice, trusting the transformative power of her parents' deep love, a curriculum tailored specifically for her and certain indifference to math-related emotional outbursts. I felt as if we had a few years at most to teach her the pleasure of doing something challenging for its own sake. It was critical that we make the right decision and that we do it quickly.

So, of course, we did nothing. We kept her in school for the rest of the year.

Even though I knew Alice wouldn't change and her teachers

weren't going to realize they were being manipulated by someone who didn't reach their armpits, I was highly anxious about my own qualifications to educate my kid—and rightfully so. Sure, I had run my mouth to friends and family about how we might try this homeschool thing at some point down the line, but that came from the same part of my brain that believes if the pilot dies and I take over the controls, I can safely land a jumbo jet. It's a fun fantasy, but the reality of either scenario conjures up outcomes that trouble the imagination.

For one thing, children who are homeschooled are frequently home. I adore my daughter in ways even my beloved words fail to express, but I was an only child; consequently, I'm a little protective of Quinn Time. Some weekends, when Alice is frolicking around the house with her father, I get confused and think: *This has been a really fun sleepover, but isn't it time for their mom to come get them?* When I read lifestyle and architecture magazines I don't daydream about the expensive furniture, elegant fixtures and opulent décor; I swoon over page after page of empty rooms. French provincial or mid-century modern, I don't care as long as it's devoid of people.

Further complicating this decision was her father, Daniel, whose clients are strewn all over the map so he frequently works from home. Could we all share the same house without one of us putting a severed head on a stake as a warning to the others? Then there was the size of the house itself. Our 1927 bungalow was ideally suited for a small family of its time. I pride myself on living in a frugal, responsible manner, which sounds better than admitting we can't afford a bigger place. Still, when a small house doubles as a schoolhouse and an office, it's fair to say Alice would get to know her parents really well. Intimately, in fact.

I wasn't sure how I felt about this.

On one hand, I think there's something valuable in knowing what your parents are truly like. Modern lives are busy and increasingly complex. Fewer than half of American families eat dinner together on any given night, tugged apart by any number of distractions—some worthwhile, others not so much. It seems perfectly reasonable to rush off to a rousing game of Wii bocce, finish a project for work or to Tweet your feelings about the Shamrock Shake, but what are we losing? My peers are reaching the age when our parents are leaving us, and I don't mean to Florida. More than once I've heard from a friend how she dearly loved her mother and father but didn't feel as if she knew them as people. Does that matter? Maybe not. The people who've shared this sentiment all seem to have grown up to be acceptably normal people. But shouldn't an important part of discovering yourself be discovering what your family was like? Whichever side you favor in the nature versus nurture argument, who your parents are certainly helped shape who you are. It would be illuminating if not downright useful to have a more rounded picture of one's parent than simply the person driving the car to lacrosse practice.

On the other hand, an adventure in home education might skew Alice's perception of her parents in unexpected directions. She would be able to say with confidence such things as "my father sometimes makes rude gestures at the phone while on conference calls and every morning he pours himself a cup of coffee and then loses it," or "my mother obsesses over social mistakes and unsuccessful jokes she made two decades ago. She also once ate an entire jar of Kalamata olives for breakfast." The shared experiences of homeschooling could inspire a closer emotional bond between our beloved child and her parents. It might also inspire a thinly veiled hope that she'd been adopted.

Through all of this dithering, my greatest fear continued to be about my optimism or, more accurately, my complete lack thereof. Of the mothers I knew who homeschooled their kids, most were either bolstered by their unyielding faith in a God who had their backs, or they were blessed with the kind of natural serenity that works to defuse normal day-to-day conflicts. One close friend who homeschooled her three kids kept telling me, "Don't worry, everything will work itself out." The only times I've ever considered using that phrase, it came out as "Everything will work itself out . . . in a really horrible way." I am more of an "It's all ashes" or "What's the point, really?" kind of person. If I had a patron saint, it would be Eeyore. We were lucky enough to be able to have the time and the resources to homeschool, but did that mean we *should* homeschool? It certainly seemed that I was designed from the ground up to hand my child over to qualified professionals so as to inflict as little harm as possible.

The bottom line, though, was that Alice's father and I both knew our daughter better than anyone and we could no longer ignore the fact that she wasn't working very hard in school. As people say when they've run out of polite variations of "slacking off," she "wasn't reaching her full potential." At the same time, I was also concerned that her homework load would increase with each passing year, leaving her less free time to follow a sudden curiosity, delve deeper into a random subject, absorb herself with a pointless activity or create something for no better reason than the muse struck her. I was greedy. I wanted her to stretch her mind and her self-confidence, but I also wanted her to play with friends, read books, listen to music and glaze over with the pleasant boredom of a long afternoon with no place to be and nothing to do.

In January, we stopped touring schools and started researching homeschool curricula. By March, I was selling Alice on the idea of homeschooling. This was fairly easy, because she wasn't entirely happy where she was. Also, I spent a lot of time pushing the "You can wake up whenever you want!" aspect. Alice, like her father, is not a morning person. I could persuade her to snake drains twelve hours a day so long as the day started at noon.

By early August, I had cobbled together a program I thought might work for us both and would meet the state of California's expectations regarding such things. For her history credits, we'd study American history, giving me the chance to be relentlessly pedantic on one of my favorite subjects while also justifying another pass through Ken Burns's *Civil War.* English would consist of studying Latin root words, reading whatever books she felt like reading and writing reviews of these books for me. Science would be an online class, which would include lectures and experiments to perform. Math would come from a series of textbooks named after one of those countries that consistently outscores America on math tests. The fact that the math course included corresponding answer keys for the instructor sealed the deal. I didn't have to be smart; I just needed to remember where I hid the answer sheets. I bought a bunch of supplies, asked Daniel to mount the whiteboard on a wall and moved Alice's globe from her closet to a prominent place in our home office.

When September rolled around again, we were in the education business.

The first day went by uneventfully. We marveled over fresh pencils, unblemished erasers and virginal workbooks. The first section of her math text included a refresher quiz that included long division with remainders. I tried to remain neutral. Alice sighed, dug in and chipped through the entire page without complaint. I barely restrained myself from fist pumps of delight. *This* was why I was meant to teach her, I thought. My child's mind would be nourished by a combination of love and structure. My positive outlook would serve as a beacon of intellectual destiny, helping her become the teenager who determines the cubic footage of the house to pass the time. If I managed this right, I'd become a mathematical embarrassment to her by spring break.

On day two, we galloped through English, talked a couple of decades of history and did some art. Actually, she did some art and I made some tea and caught up on email. We were both well served by a little break. After lunch, I brought out the math workbook and opened to the second section: fractions. Adding fractions. Subtracting fractions. Lowest-common-denominator fractions. It was a festival of fractions. Alice scowled. She put the pencil point-side down on the table and tried to make it stand up on its own. She wove the pencil through her ponytail. She tapped it like a drumstick. I encouraged her to use the pencil in the more traditional way. She excused herself for a bathroom break and didn't come back. Ten minutes later, I found her in her bedroom with a cat on her lap, reading.

"Honey," I said firmly. "You can read later. Right now is math."

"But," she said softly, "I don't know how to do fractions."

I squinted in disbelief. "You did fractions, these *exact* fractions, for a month this spring. Yes, you didn't like them, but you scored a ninety-five percent on the test. We're just making sure you remember them."

Her eyes swam with tears. "I have no idea how to do fractions. Can we just go over them? Slowly? For as long as it takes?"

I stood there in the doorway, completely flummoxed. For the first time in three years, I felt empathy for her teachers. My meticulously planned schedule danced away from me, laughing like a drunken sorority girl. In its place, Alice's schedule took over—a schedule wherein six months from now she might, grudgingly, admit that 3/4 and 6/8 were the same amount. I had made a terrible mistake and now I was going to do what my inner Nostradamus had been warning me about for years: I was going to *Break the Child*. The house, with the two of us in it, suddenly seemed both tomb empty and rush-hour full. I walked into the laundry room and sat on the floor, covered my face with my hands and pretended I was somewhere else. After a minute or so, there was a knock on the door.

"Yes?"

"Can I watch television?"

"No."

"Why not? It's not a school day."

No it wasn't, was it? The enormity of this settled on my chest like a Volkswagen, preventing me from breathing.

"Alice?"

"Yeah?"

"Do your mother a favor. Please shut the door and go back to the kitchen. Get a small paper bag from the cupboard and slide it under the door to me."

A moment later, the bag arrived. A few minutes passed. I forced myself to think of nothing but breathing into the bag in a slow and measured rhythm. The Volkswagen powered up and slowly drove off my sternum. I tried to think calm, rational thoughts. This home-school idea was a grave mistake, but I couldn't revert to Plan B. I *had* no Plan B. This horrible charade was going to have to work for the next nine months whether I was up to it or not. But what was I going to do about math? I couldn't keep bribing her with Barbies, if for no other reason than we'd run out of shelf space and our bathroom drains couldn't support that much plastic hair. How else could I convince her that fractions had a genuinely useful purpose? That *learning* about fractions had a genuinely useful purpose?

"Alice," I called into the kitchen.

"Hmmmm?" she drawled.

"How about a field trip?" I asked in an uncharacteristically cheerful tone. "A field trip to the *grocery store*!"

Without knowing it, I had stumbled upon one of the basic postulates of homeschooling: *Anything* you do with a home-schooled child outside the home can be described as a "field trip," thus rendering whatever activity you pursue a legitimate educational experience. Alice made an ambivalent noise.

"We'll get baking supplies, then we'll come home and bake," I tempted.

There was silence, followed in seconds by the sound of running feet heading toward her bedroom. Less than a minute later the kitchen door swung open. Alice was ready to go.

"Really?" she said, barely daring to breathe. I bake only under duress. Every November, I develop a tic under my right eye when the cookie-recipe Christmas magazines start piling up in the mailbox.

"Yes," I said sweetly. "I'll even let you do all the measuring."

She whooped with delight and sprinted for the garage. I went to the bathroom to brush my hair but ended up just gazing at myself in the mirror. I wondered: *Am I teaching her because she'll have to use fractions for this, or is she teaching me because we're going to end up making snickerdoodles until Easter?*

I shrugged. Either way, neither of us was crying.

Tribes

* * *

Whatever its academic benefits, that supermarket field trip got us out of the house. Eventually, I came to realize that getting out of the house is an essential aid to sanity, not only for a homeschooled child but for her parent/teacher. During the school year, Alice and I make such escapes a regular part of our routine and our lives are better for it. From three to six thirty every weekday, we take the home out of homeschooling. She has sports. She has choir. She has neighborhood friends to play with. Every day of her life, someone outside of our family is happy to see her.

And yet, wherever we go, when adults learn that Alice is being homeschooled, they react as if being told she's a shut-in. They produce a thoughtful, furrowed look and ask, "What about *socialization*?"

When you homeschool, the person standing behind you at the deli counter is concerned about your child's socialization. So are your relatives, close friends, not-so-close friends, business colleagues, ex-boyfriends, the homeless man who sits outside of the library, the UPS guy and pretty much any individual who hears your child isn't tucked in a classroom six hours a day. The lady at the dry cleaners who just a moment earlier was reenacting a recent episode of *The Biggest Loser* in great detail suddenly becomes a doctoral candidate in child development. "But what about socialization?" she will inevitably ask.

The issue seems to conjure Dickensian images. In each of these questioner's eyes, Alice sits at the window of her airless garret, plaintively gazing at a throng of children frolicking in the sunshine below. "Those other ones . . . they look like me," she whimpers to her empty room before slinking off to create conversations between her hairbrush and a wall socket.

I admit that I shared such preconceptions before we began homeschooling Alice. But now I answer the socialization question the way homeschool parents usually do: *Homeschooled kids are just as socialized as other children, maybe more so.*

Actually, I tend to just mumble unintelligibly at the questioner before scuttling away as quickly as I can. But in my mind, I spin long, impassioned, elegantly reasoned rebuttals—or rants, if you prefer. I effortlessly bring up facts from the homeschooling books I've read (Dr. Bethany Gardiner's *Highlighting Homeschooling* has a particularly good chapter on socialization). Composing these rationales can keep me up till dawn or cause me to miss my exit on the freeway. I'm incredibly verbally graceful as long as no one else is around. Here is how I imagine answering my interrogators:

"What about socialization?" Well, what about it? More specifically, what do you mean when you say "socialization"? Do you mean the Merriam-Webster definition: *A continuing process whereby an individual acquires a personal identity and learns the norms, values, behaviors and social skills appropriate to his or her social position*?

If so, great. It's an excellent definition. But it has very little to do with school.

We've been recognizably human for about fifty thousand years. For nearly all of that time, we lived in small groups, each consisting of an extended family working collectively toward the care and feeding of the clan. This tribal arrangement made sense from an evolutionary perspective because family members contain your genes, or genes pretty similar to yours, and it's in everyone's best interest to protect as many of these stress-tested genes as possible and propagate them into the next generation, right? After countless millennia of Darwinian trial and error, Homo sapiens are designed to thrive with an extended period of love and care from extended kin who maintain a vested interest in teaching us how to be productive members of a small, tightly woven community. Today, we're Facebooking, Tweeting, iProduct-pining citizens of the twenty-first century, but from the skull inward we're still refining our Stone Age brains. And the process of socialization is nowhere near complete at age five or six, when modern children start spending up to half their waking hours taking their cues from other people's children. Because they accompany their parents' daily routine, homeschooled kids spend plenty of time interacting with people of all ages, which I think most people would agree is a far more natural, organic way to socialize. Furthermore, there are scores of homeschool groups that arrange local and regional get-togethers. In most American cities, homeschool classes are available in every size and shape—so whatever you, as an amateur, cannot or should not teach, someone is probably offering a course in that subject.

You and I also know that some of the weirdest people we will ever encounter sat next to us in a classroom; they were probably born that way. Studies of identical twins raised separately indicate that much of what we think of as adapted personality is, in fact, genetic. Shy parents generally produce reserved offspring, even if the children are adopted and raised in a gregarious family. Extroverted people are more likely to have extroverted children. Homeschooling will certainly produce some socially awkward adults, but the odds are good they would have been just as quirky had they spent twelve years raising their hand for permission to go to the bathroom. In fact, quite a few kids are being homeschooled precisely because an offbeat personality tends to attract hostility. There are no bullies in homeschooling. At home you can be eccentric and survive lunch. I was a weird child, freakishly mature for my age and indifferent to what would have made me appealing to peers. And yes, I remained so despite spending most of my childhood in traditional classrooms.

Peer groups are an important part of social development. But so are older people. And babies. And cousins you get into trouble with. And great-aunts who make excellent pies. And neighbors who can fix bikes. No one looks at children in a traditional school, interacting mostly with other young people who happened to be born the same year as them, and complains of a lack of great-aunt time. But maybe they should.

Most of the homeschooled children I know have about the same amount of *after*-school peer time as the rest of the population—but, obviously, without that school day together, they do spend less time with their peers. Whether that's a good thing or a bad thing is still open to debate. The typical modern child's life is still in the beta-test stage relative to the tens of thousands of years during which socialization was accomplished the other way. The current model of school—whereby we segregate a portion of the population almost exclusively by age—is, at most, four hundred years old. Compulsory schooling in the United States is less than a hundred and fifty years old. It is, arguably, too soon to tell whether the peer group should be considered a developing child's best social influence. It's certainly an idea without precedent. Humans have historically learned to be human in a vertical process—in other words, from their elders. Schools seem to work on the assumption that we should learn how to be humans horizontally, from kids our own age because, after all, no one is better equipped to teach a fourteen-year-old boy how to be a man quite like a group of fourteen-year-old boys.

I pause to take a breath. My Imaginary Interrogator asks, "What about the homeschool families who never see other kids?"

Yeah, those families. They exist and if they were a majority of the homeschooling movement—or even a sizable percentage—I could certainly see the side of the anti-homeschooling advocates who claim that educating children at home is a form of abuse. Children who are prevented from hanging out with other children are not getting a chance to develop completely, and if I knew parents who were doing that, I'd be working my very hardest to encourage them to do things differently. Then again, if they are that disconnected from the general population, I'm probably not going to know them, am I? I'll say this: The thought of families like that troubles me, but from what I've seen and read about homeschoolers, the truly detached families are a very small percentage of the community. People make choices. Some people make terrible choices. Sterno was formulated to keep chafing dishes hot. Some people drink it. You can't condemn an entire catering practice because a few people abuse their privilege of choice.

All the homeschooling parents I know meet on a regular basis with other families. They organize field trips, cooking classes, reading clubs and Scout troops. Their children tend to be happy, confident and socially engaged.

"But," the Interrogator might ask, "how will these kids learn to deal with bullies and jerks?"

As luck would have it, there are bullies at the Scout meeting, in the mall, on the playground and even at family reunions. There are jerks everywhere you look. Children who homeschool do get to negotiate with socially toxic people. What they don't get to do is grimly endure an entire year sitting two feet away from a person who makes their lives miserable on a regular and predictable basis. It's not unreasonable to hope that by the time homeschooled children enter the world as adults, they will have acquired the self-possession required to walk away from someone who is belittling them and been spared the recurring nightmares of being trapped in the locker room with the bully.

"If you don't deal with bullies when you're young, you won't toughen up," barks Mr. Interrogator.

A recent study in the *Archives of General Psychiatry* noted a correlation between middle school bullying and later psychotic symptoms. Both the bullies and their victims exhibited higher rates of certain mental disorders. Being bullied isn't like doing bicep curls until you're able to hoist a full beer keg by yourself; being bullied is finding yourself unwillingly connected to an IV drip of acid that corrodes the most basic parts of you. There are many legitimate reasons not to homeschool. I don't think this is one of them.

"Children make friends with people unlike themselves or their families in school," says Mr. I. "This doesn't happen if you homeschool."

Please visit a local high school, either private or public, and watch the students interacting. Over there are the football players. The nerds are at the back table, playing D&D. The burnouts are behind the cafeteria, trying to make a bong out of a napkin dispenser. How many mixed groups do you actually see? Most middle schools and high schools in America have the social fluidity of Japan's imperial court.

"So, you're saying school is bad for people?"

Not at all, faithful Interrogator. Some people thrive in school; they become the best version of themselves they could possibly be. Other people wither in school; we've all seen that tragedy unfold. Most people land somewhere in the middle. As a child, Daniel sat firmly at the thriver end of the spectrum. I was more of a middler, verging on witherer. Clearly, however, school isn't the best place for every kid.

In fact, I suspect that the question, "But what about socialization?" isn't really about kids at all. It's about the social role of *parents*—specifically, about whether they can educate their kids in an age when that is generally assumed to be a task for professionals. The question behind the question is this: *"Are you up to the task of doing what your ancestors have been doing since before the discovery of fire?"*

I believe that with a little help, most people are.

Of course, this is far more than the checkout clerk wants to hear when she asks why Alice is shopping with me midmorning on a Tuesday. So I usually answer with something vague like, "Oh, she does things every day." This meets my dual criteria for a response to an ambush query: (1) It reveals nothing, and (2) it's true. Alice does *do things* every day.

At the time, however, I did find myself thinking, "Maybe the kid does need more time with her peers." Doesn't that make me sound virtuous, caring and acutely alive to my daughter's needs? I can admit something now: I usually had this thought when she was talking.

Until we started homeschooling, I'd never noticed how much of Alice's internal life was, well, external. She had meals to plan, projects to contemplate, outfits to create, old grievances to ponder, new grievances to air and paragraphs to read. All of this was out loud. I have been accused of being conversationally *generous* on occasion, but at my most voluble, I was a mere eyedropper of chatter compared to Alice's Niagara Falls. The maddening part was how Daniel could tune her right out and I couldn't. He could fold her nonstop narratives into the gentle hum of life's soundtrack, her musings no more of a distraction than the fridge running or wind rustling through the trees. There was no real harm in tuning her out. She rarely delivered any pressing information, such as, "Mom, we should probably get my leg X-rayed," or "I believe the garage is on fire." For the most part, her talking seemed to be a prophylaxis against tongue atrophy. Yet I was obliged at some cellular, maternal level to listen to every single word.

And there were so *many* of them. She could do homework and talk. She could read and talk. She talked in her sleep. At least once a day I would put up a shaky hand and mutter, "I'll be in the laundry room," where I would hide for a while, fold a few shirts and press a bag of frozen peas to my ears to reduce the swelling.

Which was where I was sitting one afternoon as I Googled: *homeschool groups Los Angeles.* I was hoping to find a tributary or two to channel her verbal surges. As luck would have it, a nearby group was having a park rendezvous the following day. Revived, I bounded in to tell Alice we'd be going out for a little while the next morning, and why. We settled in for an afternoon of her musing—out loud—over every possible outfit she might wear. I declared that "art class."

The next day, the park was full of homeschool families. Homeschooled preschoolers played happily in the sand. Homeschooled preteens created complicated games, which mostly involved running and shrieking. Homeschooled teenagers huddled in clumps by the picnic tables, muttering among themselves and practicing a moody look or two. Alice and I stood on the fringes, taking it all in. For the first time in weeks, I thought: *You know, this might work!* I could imagine her hanging out with her new homeschool friends, discussing—well, I wasn't sure what you discussed when you were a homeschool student, but it probably wouldn't be educational, so she'd be happy. I'd make all these lovely new grown-up friends—people who wouldn't begin every conversation asking about socialization—so I'd be happy. Daniel wouldn't have to hide in the garage to have a conference call, so he'd be happy. We'd all be happy. God, it was nice to feel vindicated. Alice turned to me and said, "Great. We're here." Then, after a long beat: "Now what do you want me to do?"

It was the same voice I'd heard for six months as I insisted the only reason she didn't like ballet class was that she hadn't given it enough time. (Her sixth month of ballet was her last.) "Go introduce yourself to someone," I said, pointing out a group of girls hobnobbing by a swing set. "Those girls look nice."

No child has ever voluntarily taken her mother's suggestion to go introduce herself to someone who looks nice. She sighed deeply. I sighed deeply. This wasn't working. Yes, technically we were at a group setting with other families. She was lacquered in sunblock and I was wearing actual pants, but we were still only talking to ourselves. Group-activity-wise, we might as well have been standing in our own kitchen. Within five minutes, Alice was going to suggest we leave. Of this I was certain.

Two minutes later, Alice finally said, "You know, we could just go ho—"

In desperation, I snatched her hand and dragged it toward the group of girls. She hung back in a way that signaled to any observer that I had kidnapped her from her real family—a family that never made her talk to new people—and was about to sell her into vassalage. I didn't care. It took her all of three sentences to determine these were sweet, engaging girls who had spent the better part of *their* previous day picking out park outfits. I left Alice to discuss the nuances of casual footwear and earring options while I drifted off in search of what we really came here to find that day: someone to make *me* feel better.

If you homeschool, people tend to assume things about you.

They frequently start off by assuming you're a devout Christian, or a back-to-the-land hippie, or the parent of a child who patented a search algorithm in the fifth grade. Some homeschool families are each of these things; many aren't. Some are average families, quite recognizable except for the way they educate their children. What does differentiate most homeschool families is a remarkable sense of confidence regarding their educational choice. This stands to reason because while homeschooling isn't as peculiar a choice as it might have seemed a generation ago, you're still stepping off the main path, pulling against all that societal inertia to do what everyone else does. If you feel strongly enough to make that choice, you're probably going to feel confident about the choice you've made. Unless, of course, you're me.

Here I was, standing alone in a city park on a bright Wednesday afternoon, desperately hoping someone would tell me that she, too, had spent her first month of homeschooling hiding from her child—and that it had somehow worked out beautifully. I needed a veteran of this club to approve my choices, to bolster and soothe me. This was going to be a challenge, because I am not a joiner and I am spastically self-conscious. Maybe it's the only-child thing, but put me in a group of people and I automatically start noticing the ways I'm not like them. Then again, I was nominated for an Academy Award at ten and had my tonsils out at twenty-four. The house in which I grew up had a poltergeist and had to be exorcised. In my twenties, I might have spent a week inadvertently working for organized crime. Until now, it wasn't irrational to think there weren't a lot of people out there like me. But this wasn't entirely about me anymore. This was also about Alice. It stood to reason I'd be better at educating her if I found a group of wonderful, sane people to balance out my qualities. Were the people here in this park today those people? Were these the fellow travelers who would vindicate my path and allow me to stop grinding my teeth into powder every night?

A woman I know who homeschooled her children in the 1980s told me that when they started, the homeschooling population was so small that everyone simply hung out together. Professional actors, Christian fundamentalists and families with disabled children all joined the same learning programs, shared the same activities and hit the park on the same days. By the time this woman's youngest graduated high school, however, the original group had splintered into like-minded subsets, each with its own self-reinforcing rituals and cultural biases.

I was reminded of this as I stood there on the crest of a grassy slope in Griffith Park watching sixty or so people loiter before me in the sunshine like a suburban American Seurat tableau, all the time wondering: Where was *my* tribe? And would I ever feel confident enough about homeschooling to join it if I found it?

It's harder than you might think to walk up to someone, mention how nice the weather is and segue effortlessly into a confession about one's unworthiness as a mother. I set my sights on a small, likely group, inching toward the women handing out snacks and chatting among themselves about car seats. Screwing up my courage, I introduced myself. We established that I had a daughter—the one over there with the deceptively casual but exquisitely coordinated ensemble—and that I had just started homeschooling. And then silence. I couldn't figure out a way to swing the conversation subtly around to "So, do you stop having panic attacks after the first year, or do you just drink in the daytime?"

We watched the children play for a minute or so before the conversation returned to car seats. I waited a few seconds and then drifted away.

After a few more lunges toward potential mentors, Alice caught up with me. "Are you having fun?" I asked hopefully.

"They're fine." She sighed. "Can we go home now?"

"But," I whispered sadly, "don't you have things in common?"

She shrugged. "We all homeschool. That's about it. Now, can we go? Caleb will be home soon and we've got a game planned in his yard."

A neighborhood friend trumped new homeschool friends because Alice didn't need a tribe; she already had one. For all the brave monologues I had given in my head about socialization, part of me still believed she was this unsure, socially marginalized person. No, that was me. This yearning for a group to call our own would be my adventure, not hers. If I found a group I thought would work for our family, I'd bring her along to the second meeting. But where would I find this group? This was the biggest group in L.A. and while everyone seemed lovely, I didn't think this was us. I slumped inwardly. Alone again, naturally.

Then it dawned on me. A lot has changed since the 1980s. If this wasn't the tribe I was destined to join, there was a city and a state and an entire nation filled with countless other homeschooling tribes, each with its own unique characteristics and philosophies and nothing else in common besides an active belief in home-based education. One of them would surely make me feel as if I had made the right decision for Alice.

I had some homework to do.

Magical History Tour

* * *

Before I could begin my tribal fieldwork, I had some research to do. Aside from my extremely limited experience with Alice, I knew virtually nothing about homeschooling. What was its history? What were its principles? Besides my family, the folks in Griffith Park and the people I saw online, who else was doing it? There *were* others, right?

Like most people, I had a vague sense that homeschooling began in the United States. This turned out to be correct. I also assumed that homeschooling dated to colonial times, back when free-range Pilgrims roamed New England, waiting patiently for L.L.Bean to open. I was wrong about this. My backup assumption, that homeschooling emerged during the great westward migration of the nineteenth century, was also wrong. In fact, the phenomenon we now recognize as homeschooling first showed up in 1982, the same year as the CD player. But before we discuss this radical innovation in greater depth (homeschooling, not compact discs), we should look at a few seminal events that set the stage for its emergence. Our first stop: the Protestant Reformation.

On the last day of October in 1517, a friar named Martin Luther nailed a long list of grievances on the door of a church in Wittenberg, Germany. The target of his outrage: Roman Catholic authority, which had dominated spiritual and political activity throughout Europe for a thousand years. The consequences of Luther's audacious prank so many Halloweens ago were significant, widespread and probably unintentional. In fact, an entire branch of Christianity would eventually be named after this single act of protest. The bulk of Bruder Luther's ninety-five complaints focused on the cultural and spiritual distance between Rome and the rest of Europe, but his sauerkraut was in a particular twist over the Vatican's plan to transform purgatory—or, more accurately, the avoidance thereof—into a revenue stream. Luther's arguments were detailed and varied, but two concepts are of particular interest with respect to homeschooling:

> No person is better than any other. All people can have a direct relationship with God. Neither the Pope nor any agent of his authority is more holy than any virtuous individual.

And:

> Indulgences, wherein a sinner contributes money toward the construction of St. Peter's Basilica in Rome in exchange for

preferential treatment in heaven, are irrefutable evidence of the material corruption of the Catholic hierarchy.

Across northern Europe, Christians displayed a mounting resentment toward centralized authority in general and Roman authority in particular. Within a few short years, and by virtue of a far-flung network of churches, religious schools and sympathetic bureaucrats, Luther's passion blossomed from a list of gripes to a denomination. This was a movement led by educated clerics, men who strongly believed that only by reading and understanding the Bible could devout Christians meet God's expectations of them. To their thinking, any institution that stood between man and God was an abomination; the only relationship with God was a *direct* relationship with God.

Meanwhile, over in England, King Henry VIII was having his own problems with Vatican authority. His wife, Catherine of Aragon, maintained a frustrating incapacity to bear him a live son. Henry needed a male heir because his own claim to the throne was balsa-wood flimsy and it was generally understood that a woman on the throne of England—specifically, his daughter Mary—would tempt a more powerful pretender to reclaim it. The year was 1534, another high point on the road to Reformation.

Henry had a standby womb in Anne Boleyn, but his matrimonial vows to Catherine had to be annulled by Rome before he could marry Anne "in the eyes of God" and sire a legitimate heir. The pope, no doubt acutely aware that Catherine's nephew—whose business card read "Holy Roman Emperor"—had sacked Rome the previous year and was probably looking for an excuse to sack it again, refused to grant the annulment. Never a fan of being thwarted, Henry declared himself supreme head of the Church of England. Henry was able to grant himself this promotion with relative ease because Luther's reformers had found a cordial reception on English soil, because the Catholic Church owned some of the sweetest real estate in Britain that the local nobles were happy to get their hands on, and, well, because he could.

One of his first official acts as this newly ordained pope of Canterbury was to grant himself what he wanted all along: a sanctioned annulment from Catherine. The fact that it was sanctioned by *him* was never brought up, except by a few spoilsports who more or less changed their minds once Henry had them executed. Henry's new church was sort of Protestant but sort of not. The Church of England replaced a well-dressed guy on a throne speaking directly to God in Latin with a well-dressed guy on a throne speaking directly to God in English. On the ground, not much had really changed, if you overlooked the seizure of the monasteries for the benefit of a few noble families and the fact that the head of the church could now have you tried and executed for treason as well as heresy.

As it happened, God instructed Henry to marry his hot, bun-in-the-oven Anne Boleyn so that he might legitimize the son they were destined to have. The daughter they actually *did* have, Elizabeth, was not quite male enough for Henry's taste, and about three years later God informed Henry that Anne needed to go to make room for a more heir-friendly oven. Third wife, Jane, died in childbirth, producing a child who had the good manners to be male but the poor judgment to die at sixteen. The three wives who followed didn't get pregnant. Mary, the eldest child, died without issue, so Henry *I-Speak-to-God-and-I-Ordered-a-Boy* Tudor's youngest daughter was eventually crowned Queen of England.

Good Queen Bess's relationship with both the Catholic and Protestant churches in England was pragmatic and tolerant. Most of her subjects were relieved to stop being tortured for their religious beliefs and return to healthy English pursuits like walking great distances in the rain, gardening in the mud and enjoying a nice bowl of glop. However, many Protestants still believed that God preferred strict adherence to scripture and rigid authority over tolerance. Included among this group was a notoriously fervent and unyielding sect who believed the most holy structure of faith was not the church but the *family*, and that God does not condone non-theocratic governance in any form. Needless to say, they annoyed nearly everyone who crossed their path, especially people in positions of secular authority.

In the 1650s, William Gough, one of this group's more influential pastors, wrote:

> [A] familie is a little Church, and a little common-wealth, at least a lively representation thereof, whereby triall may be made of such as are fit for any place of authoritie, or of subjection in Church or common-wealth. Or rather it is as a schoole wherein the first principles and grounds of government and subjection are learned: whereby men are fitted to greater matters in Church or common-wealth.

If you're like me and your eyes glaze over trying to read anything in Old English, with all the extra *l*'s and decorative *e*'s, the meaty bit in this quote suggests that people of God should regard their homes with the same reverence and devotion as any church or government institution. In practical terms, every family can be a little church *and* a little state but also—most important to our discussion—a little *school* where these potentially subversive concepts are reinforced from a very early age.

Still feeling a bit prickly over the Roman Catholics' *buy-your-way-out-of-hell-let's-build-a-big-cathedral* thing, these hard-core purists preferred to gather in spare, modest surroundings and express their devotion to God in small groups of like-minded souls. To them, the family was the fulcrum of the community, superseding any government or institution, especially an institutionalized church. They called themselves Puritans and, as it turned out, they liked to travel.

Let's skip forward a hundred or so years and across the Atlantic Ocean. By 1820, the New World descendants of these first Puritans have stopped calling it "schoole," they've removed the buckles from their shoes and they no longer accuse the old woman who lives down by the river of consorting with Satan and hexing their cows. In the years leading up to the Civil War, America was in the midst of its shift from an agrarian to an industrial society, and the influence of religion was being felt most specifically in social rather than political terms. Many people, especially in rural areas, taught their children at home, but the thrust of this education was the basic readin', writin' and 'rithmetic skills required to understand the gospel and manage the family's affairs. From before the Revolutionary War, the sons of the ruling class and affluent merchants were sent to private schools in New England or, if they could afford it, all the way back to Old England for a proper gentleman's education. During this time, a nascent middle class emerged whose children received community-funded education in local schoolhouses, schoolhouses that were typically little and occasionally red. Also at this time, during the early days of America's urban expansion, the poorest children were often sent to "parochial" schools, which came into existence as part of the Catholic Church's mandate to better address the needs of its most disadvantaged parishioners and to make an investment in the future welfare, and wealth potential, of its expanding flock.

In 1852, Massachusetts was the first state to make attending school mandatory for children between the ages of eight and fourteen, for at least three months out of every year. This was hardly a recipe for advanced scholarship—I've spent more time trying to learn how to use a new can opener—but it was a game-changer. For the first time in history, the children of middle- and working-class citizens had free access to a state-funded education. These first efforts represented an unprecedented commitment of government treasury toward public education and government influence over its execution.

By 1918, every state in America had some requirement for compulsory education, though it must be noted that the motivations for this plunge into social engineering were not entirely altruistic. The state didn't want scholars; it wanted workers. Waves of immigrants were arriving in the United States, not only from familiar places like England and Germany, but from Russia, Ireland, Italy, Sweden, the hodgepodge of eastern Europe and even China. Employers needed these new arrivals literate and numerate—educated enough to read an instruction manual, follow a diagram and operate a machine in the factories that were sprouting up all over America.

Mandatory education was also the pet cause of impassioned social reformers such as A. Bronson Alcott (Louisa May's father), Henry David Thoreau and, a few decades later, John Dewey—men who believed the true foundation of a nation of equals was its classrooms. It appealed as well to anti-immigrant types who saw the newcomers as dangerously alien and wanted to make them more like *us*. The net effect was one of those rare moments in American history when liberals and conservatives found something to agree upon. The next thing you know, school bells were ringing everywhere.

Which circles us back to religion. The education offered by America's public schools was secular in theory (thanks to the First Amendment), and becoming ever more so in practice. This didn't sit well with some of the Puritans' spiritual heirs, men who had never quite gotten comfy with all that Age of Enlightenment stuff—and who were as suspicious of government institutions as their forebears had been during the reign of Elizabeth I. The consensus over mandatory schooling began to fray in the 1920s as conservative evangelicals sought to protect young minds from creeping godlessness. They began to articulate their concern that a public education was designed to create within the students an allegiance to their government instead of their families and their Christian beliefs.

In 1925, Tennessee legislators passed fundamentalist-backed legislation banning the teaching of Darwin's theory of evolution in public schools. A high school science teacher named John Scopes was arrested for defying the new law. For those of us who share the same cinema-infused reference points, Spencer Tracy's—I mean Clarence Darrow's—client *lost* the Monkey Trial and was fined one hundred dollars by the Rhea County court. For the anti-evolutionists, this was as good as it was going to get. The verdict was later overturned on a technicality. Over the next decade, forty-one bills or resolutions were put before various state governments to outlaw the teaching of evolution but, of these, only Mississippi and Arkansas were able to pass legislation fueled by creationist sentiment. By 1939, evolution was being taught in most, if not all, public high schools in America.

In 1958, the National Defense Education Act was signed into law, providing federal funding for American education on all levels. The stated reason for the act was to support the growing number of students hoping to attend college. The fact that the Soviet Union had launched *Sputnik* the previous autumn and was probably looking down at us from space with unblinking Communist eyes might have had something to do with its speedy passage. One by-product of the NDEA was a mountain of textbooks, produced under the auspices of the American Institute of Biological Sciences, which stressed the importance of evolution as the unifying principle of biology.

In 1962, the U.S. Supreme Court declared it unconstitutional for state officials to compose an official prayer and require its recitation in public school (*Engel v. Vitale*). In 1963, the Court ruled that sponsored Bible readings were, likewise, unconstitutional on public school property (*Abington v. Schempp*). If you were the sort of person who put God first in your life, it became pretty clear your government wasn't going to backstop your spiritual convictions, at least not during school hours.

By the end of the 1960s, Christian fundamentalists were feeling demoralized. They'd spent the previous decade losing every cultural touchstone they assumed to be safe. First the schools pushed out God. Then the federal government ratified the eviction. The whole country, meanwhile, had thrown itself into a debauch of sex, dope and pelvically oriented music. The mainstream Protestant denominations seemed to have abandoned all efforts to counter these tendencies, so disgruntled conservatives migrated to sterner, if fringier, sects. Their influence over American education reached an all-time low.

The tide began to turn in 1976, when a Baptist minister named Jerry Falwell produced a series of rallies called "I Love America," based on the proven methods of the revival meeting. Reverend Falwell believed the moral fabric of the United States had slipped so far into decay that he could no longer endorse the longstanding Baptist tradition of separating the pulpit from the polling booth. Within three years he created the Moral Majority, an enthusiastic group of politically active Christian conservatives who campaigned on issues near and dear to Falwell's vision of faith and morality.

Falwell's success encouraged like-minded leaders. In March 1980, an evangelical psychologist named Dr. James Dobson started a fifteen-minute radio show dedicated to teaching parents how to raise and govern their families in accordance with a strict and literal interpretation of the Bible. Within a year, *Focus on the Family* was broadcast in more than a hundred major radio markets in the

United States. In 1982, Dobson interviewed Dr. Raymond Moore, an educator who had written a book called *Better Late Than Early*, which advocated family-centered education and the even more provocative theory of delaying all formal education until the child is ready, which might not be until the age of ten or twelve depending on the child and his environment. What mainstream experts thought about this theory wasn't relevant because, as William Gough and his Puritan colleagues preached three centuries earlier, the family united under a literal reading of the Bible comes first.

Until this point, homeschooling in the United States existed in small pockets, mostly practiced by proto-survivalists, freethinking hippies and other outsiders whose endorsement the fundamentalists were probably eager to avoid. Dobson's interview with Moore changed all that. By the late 1980s, fundamentalist ministers were directing parents to "bring their children home," while citing relevant passages from the Bible:

> And all thy children shall be taught of the LORD; and great shall be the peace of thy children. —Isaiah 54:13

> And, ye fathers provoke not your children to wrath: but bring them up in the nurture and admonition of the Lord.
> —Ephesians 6:4

> And these words, which I command thee this day, shall be in thine heart: And thou shalt teach them diligently unto thy children, and shalt talk of them when thou sittest in thine house, and when thou walkest by the way, and when thou liest down, and when thou risest up. —Deuteronomy 6:6–9

> Casting down imaginations, and every high thing that exalteth itself against the knowledge of God, and bringing into captivity every thought to the obedience of Christ.
>
> —2 Corinthians 10:5

These passages, which have existed in one form or another for two millennia, did not lead to homeschooling in Sweden or Spain or Prussia. It happened in the United States, a place where fiercely devout, hierarchy-loathing European Protestants—people who placed a high priority on literacy and individualism—founded a civilization that bears their imprint to this day. America was the first country to have religious liberty written into its operating system, and the first to experience three "Great Awakenings"—waves of religious fervor so intense that historians study them like dynasties or wars—in as many centuries. It's also the country that invented the pioneer spirit. If you don't like what's happening in your town, or your school, you light out for the territory.

In 1993, responding to a case brought by a fundamentalist lobbying group, the state supreme court of Michigan declared homeschooling legal under the First Amendment. This precedent has been used to effectively caponize any further efforts to outlaw homeschooling in the United States. Reverend Gough must have been smiling in his grave.

(Anyone who knows the story of homeschooling's origins just read this and flinched at how much I skipped over. I totally agree; there wasn't room to tell the story fully. If you're interested in the topic, I think Milton Gaitner's *Homeschooling: An American History* is the best book out there.)

Over a decade later, it was starting to emerge that homeschooling was no longer the exclusive province of Christian conservatives and countercultural outliers. Parents were simply looking for other means to educate their kids; and I was Exhibit A. To get a handle on the current demographics, I closed the books and opened the search engine. My first question for the online oracle: How many homeschoolers are there?

A cornucopia of statistics spilled from my laptop. I learned that the 2000 census estimated there were 1,096,000 children homeschooling in the United States. That number was projected to reach 1.9 million by 2010, and some homeschool advocates expect it to surpass 2.5 million by 2014.

Today, according to the National Household Education Survey, 3 percent of America's school-age population is being educated at home. If you include students participating in online charter schools (which don't count as homeschooling in most surveys), that number is closer to 4 percent. To give this some perspective, there are more homeschoolers relative to the general population of school-age Americans than there are self-identified Jews in the general population (2.2 percent) but fewer than the number of left-handers (8.5 percent). Someone who enjoys statistical math can calculate the odds of meeting a left-handed Jewish homeschooler.

From 1998 to 2007, the annual growth rate of families choosing to homeschool has averaged somewhere between 7 percent and 15 percent. A spread of eight percentage points represents a margin of error so wide even a statistical nitwit like me couldn't fail to notice, but this is due less to flaws in data analysis than flaws in data collection.

In fact, all the homeschooling stats cited above are a little shaky. It's hard to measure the homeschooling population with any precision, in part because a sizable segment of that population tends to avoid such things as polls and surveys. Exactly how big is this wary subset? Good luck finding that out. When I attended my first fundamentalist homeschooling convention, the woman at the sign-in desk asked me if I wanted to be on their mailing list. I gladly added my name to the roster, but first I asked my usual question: "Do you sell your mailing list?"

The woman clutched her neck and gasped, "Oh my, no! We *never* give out information!" Then she leaned in closer to explain, "We have members who home-birth and refuse to file birth certificates for their children. We are very respectful of personal freedom." So, to all the social scientists out there: If you're curious about how many Americans refuse to file birth certificates, I wish you luck with your research. Don't use my name.

For those of us who do consider such things as bench warrants, one question tends to pop up early in the process: Is it even legal to homeschool your child in the United States? The answer: Yes. No. Maybe. Seven states are highly regulated, each requiring state certification for the parents and a preapproved curriculum for each student. Eighteen states are less rigorous, requiring notification of homeschooling and a year-end evaluation by a certified professional. Thirteen states only require the parents notify the local school board that they plan to homeschool, and ten states require no notice whatsoever. If you're planning a sixth-grade curriculum built around the cinematic oeuvre of Rob Zombie or koi-pond architecture, I suggest moving to Indiana or New Jersey, because North Dakota won't allow it.

Here is a list of the states and their relative degree of permissiveness (or lack thereof) regarding homeschooling. I must confess I was surprised by where some states showed up on this list. Strange bedfellows, indeed.

High Regulation: The following states require parents to send notification or achievement test scores and/or professional evaluation, plus other requirements (e.g., curriculum approval by the state, teacher qualification of parents or home visits by state officials): MA, ND, NH, NY, PA, RI and VT.

Moderate Regulation: The following states require parents to send notification, test scores and/or professional evaluation of student progress: AR, CO, DC, FL, GA, IA, LA, MD, ME, MN, NC, OH, OR, SC, SD, TN, VA, WA, WV and the U.S. Virgin Islands.

Low Regulation: The following states require parental notification only: AL, AZ, CA, DE HI, KS, KY, MS, MT, NE, NM, NV, UT, WI, WY and the territories of American Samoa and the Northern Mariana Islands.

No Regulation: The following states have no requirement for parents to initiate any contact: AK, CT, ID, IL, IN, MI, MO, NJ, OK and TX. Also Puerto Rico and Guam.

If you prefer to dispense with regulations altogether, Guam and Puerto Rico don't even require state exams to graduate (perhaps because they're not actually states). It should also be noted that they have delightful tropical climates.

What about the expatriate route? Is homeschooling legal in

other countries? Here again, the answer is: Yes. No. Maybe. For example, homeschooling is legal in France but, as to be expected from the nation that gave us the word "bureaucracy," there are examinations to assure the matriculation of proud, productive *jeunes citoyens* who can distinguish a well-made baguette.

The People's Republic of China does not allow homeschooling for its citizens but does allow it for foreign students. Perhaps they're hoping more parents like me will end up teaching math, creating another generation of staggering indebtedness.

Hong Kong, on the other hand, doesn't allow homeschooling at all. Neither do Spain, Sweden, Germany and Greece. It is legal pretty much everywhere else in the world, sometimes with conditions, often not. I was shocked, however, to discover that homeschooling is not allowed in the Netherlands. I could only imagine that after legalizing pot, prostitution and gambling, they had to outlaw something.

Unchartered Territory

* * *

After a couple of months of homeschooling, I took stock. On the plus side, our house was less stressful—if for no other reason than the elimination of the daily "GET IN THE CAR RIGHT NOW! YOU'RE GOING TO BE LATE FOR SCHOOL! HERE, TAKE THIS WASHCLOTH AND WASH YOUR FACE IN THE REARVIEW MIRROR AT STOPLIGHTS!" ceremony. Just as I'd intended, my daughter was getting the opportunity to explore interests for as long as she saw fit. In fact, for several days I had been banging my shin against the old wooden box of fabric samples that had been dragged out so she could create a line of resort wear for the cats. She was reading. She was grudgingly doing a little math. She was creating cat couture. She was happy.

On the minus side, there was what I now describe as the Portugal Problem. Not long after our homeschool year had started, Alice vaulted happily into the kitchen and stuck a book under my nose. "I found a mistake," she chirped. Alice loved finding spelling and grammar mistakes printed in books. I believe it confirmed her suspicions that adults are born middle-aged without actually having learned anything at all. I inspected the page and looked at her blankly. She sighed and pointed at a sentence. "It says the country of Portugal! They think Portugal is a country!" she added and cackled in delight.

I asked carefully, "When, in fact, it's a . . . ?"

"State in Italy!" she hooted.

Oh, dear. I'm not sure other preadolescent American children even consider Portugal at all. Maybe they think it's where the video game *Portal* originated. But the fact remains: Portugal is a country. Also, Italy doesn't have states. I don't know what Italy does have exactly, but it's not states. Alice looked disappointed and beetled off to uncover more human ineptitude. Every day after this chance encounter between my daughter and the Iberian Peninsula, I'd think about poor misplaced Portugal. I'd caught this one, but what else was I missing? Did she think the Wars of the Roses involved aphids? Did she believe proper nouns wore white gloves and top hats? Did she think the food pyramid was designed by the Egyptians? Was her future being compromised by a parent/teacher who wasn't completely certain what Italy *had* in place of states? Was there some way we could homeschool but still provide her with a solid catalog of basic elementary school facts? Was there a way to give her the kind of education that would allow her to follow her unique inclinations but still spot Portugal on a map of Europe? It turns out, maybe there was.

Which is how we ended up getting eight boxes of free educational material in the mail. Free to me, anyway. If you're reading this and you are a California taxpayer, you paid for it; thank you very much. Being as I'm a taxpayer, I guess I paid for a bit of it. You also paid for a little plastic flute—called a "recorder" for no logical reason—that my child uses primarily to generate random shrieks of noise and terrorize the dog.

I didn't pay for that part.

This bountiful cache of educational stuff came as the result of my enrolling Alice in an online charter school overseen and funded by the Los Angeles Unified School District. Since Alice was officially attending a public school, I would be legally responsible for making sure she learned everything her peers were learning. Since we were at home, she could learn all these things without ever having to find her shoes. Considering that every time we needed to leave the house her shoes somehow fled to the Italian state of Portugal, this arrangement showed promise.

Along with eight cartons full of books and tapes and science-y bits came the mandatory schedule and the paperwork. Legally, Alice had to be in school six hours a day. The charter school certainly couldn't come into my house and confirm we were following this directive, but they gave me a suggested schedule for each day, each week and each month. If we followed their schedule, Alice would be in school six hours a day. We were allowed to switch some of the subjects around a bit so she could do art for three days running if she felt so inclined, but at some point she'd have to stop drawing her Gauguin studies and complete the 260 minutes of math required every week. (That's four and one-third hours, for those of you who don't have a calculator handy.) If Alice and I wanted to bake cookies and talk about measuring cups and fractions, I assume the charter school would be pleased for us in the abstract, but this would not count as math time. Worksheets counted as math time.

This rigid adherence to a timetable, I've come to find out, is why online charter schools make some homeschool parents crazy. Between the lack of parental choice and the invisible, omniscient principal guiding your hand toward routine assignments, some don't even consider charter programs to be homeschooling. To them, it's just relocation. In the beginning, I was less troubled by the specter of Big Ed in my house than my inability to hide the recorder between cacophony lessons. That was just what my house needed: a horror-film soundtrack running endlessly in the background.

Very quickly, our new pedagogical plan developed cracks. First, and to no one's surprise, Alice was less interested in doing math than creating art; and she was less interested in creating her own state-mandated version of a Calder mobile than she was in using her publicly funded construction paper to wallpaper the doghouse. She was learning, maybe. I was screaming, silently. The English lessons were so basic that Alice took to flipping through a magazine while doing them, but the syllabus would absolutely not let her work outside her grade. Finally, there was the teacher assigned to us. Or rather, there was a name and an email address to which I sent daily questions about where to send the schoolwork or when to arrange our compulsory meeting without ever getting a response. In just a few weeks, we'd generated stacks of assignments that Alice had grudgingly created, but we had no one to send them to. This was, indeed, disconcerting but manageable. What wasn't manageable was "Rocky Mountain High."

Part of Alice's educational material was an audiocassette of songs she was instructed to memorize for music class. My first thought at the time was, *I wish we hadn't just thrown out those five useless audiocassette players, but at least she didn't get another recorder.* So I bought a cassette player. On the second day, we listened to the music for the sanctioned period of time. One of the songs was "Rocky Mountain High." This was not the John Denver standard, which, although a bit dopey, maintains a certain classic durability. Oh, no. This is a drab little dirge written by a third-grader with lyric deficiency syndrome and a fondness for de-winging houseflies. It goes something like this:

Rocky mountain, rocky mountain, rocky mountain high.
When you're in that rocky mountain, hang your head and cry.
Do, do, do, do, do remember me.
Do, do, do, do, do remember me.

It's the kind of song a child learns in a single hearing. It's the kind of song a child unconsciously hums for hours at a stretch. It's the kind of song where I'd have gladly mixed equal parts Jack Daniel's and laudanum to uncoil it from my brain. This "Rocky Mountain High" acted as a sort of reverse epidural, numbing me to all sensation and blocking out any sort of awareness from the neck up. If this wretched little ditty was indicative of what the LAUSD thought my family needed, it bore consideration that the curriculum was crafted by someone I used to date, and it had ended badly.

At times it seemed that the entire experience of an online charter school was an *Incredible Journey*–ish slog through the digestive system of a dying bureaucracy. So it's not surprising to admit the final straw was, well, a pain in the butt. After six weeks in this program, I got a snippy email from the heretofore silent teacher, informing me that if we continued to fail to submit Alice's schoolwork or arrange a parent/teacher meeting, Alice would have to repeat this year of school. The teacher had cc'd the head of the program. At first I panicked because I'm me and everything is my fault and shame is always just one email away. Then I squinted. I knew this letter. This was a cover-your-ass letter. It dawned on me that because we'd started after the school year had officially begun, we had been assigned to someone who already had her hands full. Teachers at online charters, I later learned, can be assigned up to fifty students to manage at a time. I guessed that she had completely forgotten about Alice until the previous day, when her superior asked about the missing child. I understood and I sympathized. Hey, I've written a CYA letter or two myself over the years. But for someone teaching online, she was pretty naive about how email worked. I cheerfully wrote back, attaching every single email I had sent over the previous six weeks asking for help. I also made sure to cc the head of the program—whose email address she'd so generously provided. Some rocky mountaineer might hang her head and cry, but it wouldn't be me. The next day I filled out the mountain of paperwork it took to un-enroll Alice from the online charter school.

I wouldn't say the program was a complete waste of time; it

taught me that our family was probably not ideally suited for a highly structured curriculum. We went back to the cobbled-together program I had created back in the summer. As for Portugal, I bought a placemat for Alice with all the countries of Europe. I bought one for myself, too.

And the doghouse has never looked better.

Joy Story

* * *

So when you're me and you've spent the past several weeks accounting for every second of your child's intellectual development in a state-supervised charter school, what starts to sound damned good? Unschooling! That's what.

If this is your first trip to the academic rodeo, let me give you the rundown on unschooling. In the 1970s, a teacher named John Holt put forth the theory that education as it was being conducted in most schools in America was counter to the ways humans actually learn. Humans learn not through rote repetition, memorizing facts and filling in workbooks, but through passion, through trial and error, through working on a problem until we either master it or run out of interest. Over time, Holt's model of education was dubbed *unschooling*. In 1991, John Taylor Gatto, soon to become the reigning prophet of unschooling, gave a speech that took Holt's message several steps further. At its core, Gatto's speech attacked the fundamental model of modern education as being inherently insane. Public schools weren't arranged to teach children but to house them. A well-trained student, he charged, panders to authority, shows no initiative and obeys meaningless orders. Gatto claimed science classes were no longer creating scientists, history classes weren't creating statesmen and writing classes weren't creating poets. What was being created? Automatons perfectly designed to work for large corporations that created products and services that other automatons would desire to own or use in place of pursuing a meaningful life. In Gatto's view, school wasn't just unproductive—it was actively malignant. Modern schools create shallow-thinking, grade-grubbing, intellectually and emotionally dependent drones. Gatto wrapped up his speech saying, "School is a twelve-year jail sentence where bad habits are the only curriculum truly learned." To which he added, "I teach school and win awards doing it. I should know."

What made these comments all the more remarkable was that they were part of John Taylor Gatto's acceptance speech as New York City's Teacher of the Year—an award he'd achieved three years in a row. I'm guessing that after he finished, there was a new standard for the phrase "awkward silence." But theatrical timing aside, I couldn't exactly disagree with the man. There were simply too many examples of the educational system missing the evidence of its own failures.

Take school hours. Study after study has proven what parents could have told you for free: Teenagers don't do mornings. At some point during early adolescence, a teenager's brain temporarily rewires itself with new instructions to stay up late and sleep in the next morning. This alteration is neither cultural nor social. It's biological. Some behaviorists theorize that part of what we've come to think of as disruptive adolescent behavior—rudeness, mood swings, lack of focus—might actually be the symptoms of chronic sleep deprivation. When a few school districts experimented with starting high school an hour or so later, everything measurable improved: grades, attitude, behavior. And yet most high schools won't even consider starting later. Why? Because most school systems use the same buses for all the grades they serve. School administrators need the high school students dropped off early enough to give the bus drivers adequate time to deliver the younger kids to and from their classes. Also, teachers—most of whom are adults—prefer the early-in, early-out schedule, and the current schedule is more in line with the work hours of the parents. This makes sense on any number of practical levels, but when it comes to actually teaching teenagers, we end up with No Child Left Awake.

And then there's testing. Most parents who live in a school district with standardized testing will tell you these tests have little to do with the betterment of their children. Teachers whose classes are tested against a statistical norm tend to spend the better part of the school year preparing their students for the test, which isn't quite the same thing as educating them. Countless books, articles and studies have tracked how irrelevant and even detrimental standardized testing is for most students. One study even indicates that children who do test well have a propensity for shallow thinking.

So if standardized testing isn't for the children, who is it for?

Certainly not the teachers. Someone who became a teacher because of a passion to, you know, *teach* is horrified to find herself having to cram predigested curricula into not-so-eager minds with the desperate urgency of a foie gras goose farmer. To Gatto, the only real beneficiaries are the bureaucrats who have created an educational system that allocates six hours a day, five days a week, nine months a year to teaching things that either are irrelevant or could be taught in a fraction of the time at a fraction of the cost. He believes that basic literacy and numeracy can be taught in a hundred hours—the trick is knowing *when* the child is ready to start the process. If the student comes to it naturally, she will develop an effortless affinity for words and numbers that will prepare her for a lifetime of continuous learning. Considering the number of seemingly indestructible industries that have imploded over the past few years, it's safe to assume that, going forward, anyone who hopes to earn a living is going to need to keep learning and adapting to change throughout his or her career. Why, then, are we spending our limited resources preparing our children for tests when we could be encouraging them to be curious and fearless learners? Why are we stuffing their heads with data instead of helping them acquire useful skills? There were many points to Gatto's argument and I was beginning to find myself nodding at least once a page as Alice flipped through Gatto's book next to my bed and saw an even sharper point.

"So, if we do this unschooling thing, I can read whatever I want. And I never ever have to do math again? *Ever?*"

"Honey, I don't think that's what Mr. Gatto is saying here, but I guess some people could do tha—"

"*Yes!* In your *face*, factoring!" Many fist pumps and Kabuki snarls ended the discussion for the moment.

Factoring had become an issue. Alice didn't see any reason to break down numbers into smaller numbers. To her way of thinking, we were somehow just encouraging these odious numbers to breed. I would explain how we were warming up her brain for the wild ride that was algebra. She, of course, would ask what the point to algebra was, exactly. After a pause and a quick coughing fit to inspire pity, I'd tell her algebra helped prepare her mind for calculus. At which point she would ask when we could start unschooling.

And that, ultimately, was my biggest concern with unschooling. The last part of the developing human brain to come online is the part that can predict consequences. If I allowed Alice to take the lead on her own education right now, there was a real possibility she'd miss out on critical educational milestones. The Alice of January couldn't imagine how the Alice of May might have different passions and interests, let alone the Alice of 2022. I had a friend whose daughter hated Algebra I but fell in love with Algebra II, eventually getting so good at mathematics that she majored in engineering at a top-notch university. To me, the difference between Algebra I and Algebra II was "Thing stuck to the bottom of your shoe" and "Thing stuck to the bottom of your shoe on a hot day," but my friend's daughter, this soon-to-be engineer, found great joy in Algebra II. Had this girl been allowed to stop after Algebra I—or halfway through Algebra I, as she had frequently begged her mother—she never would have learned the subtle delights of hideously unattractive numbers with Greek symbols and tiny exponents waggling lewdly at their extremities.

Besides, wasn't an important part of education to sometimes experience the joy that comes from doing something you love and at other times experience the joy of getting that miserable bastard of a chore behind you? Even the most wonderful adult activity has its sloggy bits. Maybe part of the big lesson of education is to try our hardest even when we're not delighted with the assignment. If everyone unschooled, would we evolve into a nation of songwriters and hip-hop dancers lined up to see that single insurance claims adjustor, that one dentist, that lone clerk at the courthouse? Then again, by staying within a fairly traditional academic model, was I insisting that Alice be unhappy merely as practice for future unhappiness? If experiencing misery built character, I could be building *my* character by letting her sing an endless rondo of "Rocky Mountain High" from the backseat.

Maybe Gatto was right. Maybe the system was insane and not conducive to learning. Or maybe I was right when I suspected that Alice, if she chose her own educational path, would spend the rest of her childhood reading science fiction and creating formal wear for cats. Were we to try unschooling, my hope would be that science fiction led inevitably to science fact; that her innate scholar would be pushed to the surface by virtue of her own passion and curiosity. I don't know about the migration from fiction to physics in Alice's case, but I'm confident her cats would have the proper wardrobe to attend the ceremony at the Royal Swedish Academy of Sciences, should the Nobel Prize show up in our mailbox.

Also, there was this thing I couldn't quite get around with Gatto. I empathized with his concerns about the educational system in which he taught, but after a few hundred pages I noticed his contempt extending to include government, large-scale organizations and anything compulsory. His musings about a free-market educational system took on a messianic timbre, as did his prediction that if it the system were established to his liking, the resulting population would be so highly motivated and autonomous it would render the legal, judicial and psychiatric professions obsolete.

I began to realize these conversations had a familiar reverb. I'd heard similar ideas somewhere before, but where? A few pages later, it suddenly hit me: Gatto was a Libertarian. Several of my friends' first husbands were Libertarians. Many, many times I have experienced the subtle joy of listening to someone spend an entire evening describing how the world would be a better place if we privatized something large and unwieldy like the police department or the water utility or the Philippines. I've generally found Libertarians to be a well-read, impassioned group of people, but never once have I heard one say, "You know, there might be another side to this story," or "No, in fact, none of my ideas have ever been tried out in a world with actual people in it," or "Hey, I've been going on about disbanding NASA for almost an hour; what's going on in *your* life?" Of course, any conversations I've had with a Libertarian tended to stay in the shallow side of the pool, which is to say the theoretical side. I can't recall having had a discussion about a real Libertarian state because, to the best of my knowledge, there has never been a real Libertarian state, with the possible exception of Somalia.

Free-market politics aside, Gatto's principles are shaped around an ideal society closely modeled after the agrarian, small-business, family-centric world of postcolonial America. Education as we know it today may be a largely failed experiment, but at least we have a century of data to work with. Gatto's followers are proposing we return to a social contract last in place when smallpox was an issue. Things are different now—very different—and, as with most critical decisions facing us these days, Gatto's supporters and detractors are divided into armed camps. I didn't know if it was in my daughter's best interest to become a lab rat for either side of this debate.

And yet, there was just enough meat on some of these arguments that I was compelled to see if there was anything in this unschooling philosophy that might work for us. One problem was that I couldn't figure out a way to dabble in it. Either I agreed with the underlying principle and let my child learn as she would, or I didn't and found another educational path. It seemed to me you could no more be a part-time unschooler than you could be a part-time giraffe. If we did it, we'd have to go all-in. This frightened me but also appealed to me because I am fascinated by people with strong convictions. My family crest consists of a chewed cuticle and a furrowed brow set on a field of beige question marks. People who know with absolute certainty how things in life should be are catnip to me. Research must be done. To the Internet!

In website after website, scores of unschooling families lined up neatly for inspection, and they appeared to be a crafty lot. Here was an unschooling family showing off their weaving. Here was one with homemade ceramic wind chimes. Here was one daughter making all the family's clothes. Another canned vegetables for the pure joy of it. Oooh, and so much animal husbandry. There were pygmy goats and 4-H rabbits and heirloom pigs and llama farms, but mostly there was poultry. I saw more chickens in thirty minutes than I've seen in three decades. If nothing else, it seems to unschool is to never suffer the taste of a store-bought egg.

If having domesticated fowl in one's backyard was a mandatory component of unschooling, we might have to move along. Not that I didn't want chickens. Believe me, with the expanse of clothing line-drying greenly in the backyard and my new habit of wearing pajama-shaped pants until dusk, it wasn't as if I feared becoming more unkempt. No, the chicken veto would not have come from me. About a year earlier, when the economy was trying out new ways to sink even lower and everyone was getting that apocalyptic gleam, I asked Daniel in my most carefully casual tone, "What would you say to my putting a coop in the backyard and raising a couple of chickens?"

He turned the page of his magazine and said evenly, "The day after the chickens arrive, I'll put a '64 Pontiac up on blocks in the front yard." He was not joking.

I stared at Daniel while he serenely continued to read. "What hurts is how quickly you answered." I pouted. "It's like you've been waiting for this."

He leaned over and kissed me sweetly. "Of course I have. And that also goes for geese, rabbits and cows."

Then, one late night while I was trying to find a group of craft-fearing, poultry-free unschoolers with whom I could identify online, I stumbled across a subspecies called "Radical Unschoolers." As it sounds, Radical Unschooling is an extension of the basic unschooling model taken to the extreme. If unschooling was, as they believed, the best way to learn, then wasn't it also the best way to live? Intriguing. What?

When children reach a certain age, most of them end up noticing the universal inequity of youth: "There's a Mother's Day and a Father's Day, so why isn't there a Child's Day?" To which most parents answer, "Because every day is Child's Day; finish your lima beans." The average American child certainly has an awful lot of sweet stuff to be grateful about; many have more objects and opportunities than their grandparents could have dreamt up. But the average American child also has schoolwork to worry about, and chores, climate change, backpack-induced scoliosis, global terrorism, school bullies and lima beans. To the Radical Unschoolers, every day really is Child's Day. Radically unschooled children are allowed to live each day in freedom, being exactly who and what they are at that moment. They have no bedtime, no mandatory foods, no off-limit words. If your child is tender-headed and shrieks like a parrot when her hair is brushed, the Radical would suggest you not brush her hair. If she prefers to let it mass into a giant dreadlock that collects food and gnats, well, it's really not your problem, is it? After all, it's not your hair; it's hers. The basic operating principle of Radical Unschooling is that you should not treat a child any differently than you would treat another adult, which is to say without guilt, coercion or threats.

I found this entirely fascinating, at least in part because many of my adult relationships are powered by guilt, coercion and threats. It also sounded vaguely familiar: children addressing their parents on a first-name basis, the high percentage of purple clothing, the mystifying need to describe one's highest state of being as "actualized." I had the creeping sensation I'd seen this all before. And then it dawned on me: This was parenting in 1970s Los Angeles. I had a fair number of grade-school classmates who smelled like Fritos because their parents believed bathing them against their will would crush their spirit. They also smelled like Fritos because they had chosen to only eat Fritos and drink Tab for a week. I wondered what any of today's Radical Unschooling parents would say when I told them one of my more actualized classmates grew up to start a cult and another manages a hedge fund.

Several mouse clicks later, I learned that the Radical Unschoolers were going to have a conference! No, that couldn't be right. A conference is, by definition, hierarchical and structured. Perhaps on the first day we'd vote for a less dead-white-Eurocentric-male way to describe it. Sure enough, two pages later the website promised not workshops, because . . . well, you know, *work*shops, with that tricky word, *work*, sucking all the happiness out of the room. Instead, we'd experience four days of *joy*shops. We'd be *joying* on Tibetan prayer flags. We'd be *joying* with Hula-Hoops. We'd be *joying* ourselves to a frazzle at a Sister Goddess Party. The website itself was fairly restrained but I knew with absolute conviction that the person who typed the event listings had been wearing lavender oil, batik and something fair trade and itchy. The event promised to be a "convergence of wisdom sharing and happy learning for everyone." Maybe. For me it was a perfect excuse to make Daniel the primary educator for three days, which increased the odds of wisdom sharing and happy learning in Los Angeles, at least.

As always with such things, there were a few wrinkles. I'd have to travel to the East Coast and stay for a couple of days. I hate travel. First of all, I have to hold the plane in the air by sheer force of will because I don't see how something that heavy can stay in the air. I suspect it's only our collective belief in it that's keeping it up—like Tinker Bell—and my terrible knowledge of this fact will cause the plane to plummet to Earth. Between digging my fingers into the armrest and not screaming from the moment the engines start until I'm in the luggage area, airplane travel exhausts me. Then I'd have to rent a car and drive on roads I don't know, where there might possibly be weather unlike what I'm accustomed to in Los Angeles, which is to say any weather at all. Also, there would be tollbooths and what if I ran out of change? Would I have to live there at the tollbooth until I panhandled enough change from passing motorists? Would the tollbooth attendants mock me? Should I prepare a sign that said "Ignorant Californian Needs Spare Change for Tolls" and pack it in my luggage? And then if I somehow managed to survive the flight and the strange-road driving and possible weather and the tollbooths, I'd arrive at another hotel where they'd give me a key card and I'd spend the next four days trying to get into my room.

This was not an irrational fear. You can hand ninety-nine people a key card and within a minute they'll be dumping their luggage on the extra double bed. Give me the same key and be prepared to watch twenty minutes of my impotently plunging the card into the door. I assume it's the same electromagnetic quirk that prevents automatic hand dryers from recognizing the fact I'm waving my wet hands in front of them. More than once, I've had to ask a stranger to activate the hand dryer in a public bathroom. Could I convince a stranger to let me into my room? Was that a wise idea? Isn't this the sort of thing people do about a week before their body is found in a culvert? And even if I do convince a benign stranger to let me into my room, what if there's someone hiding in the closet? Unlike key card anxiety, there is no legitimate basis for this fear. All the times I've been coaxed to travel on my own there has never, not once, been someone hiding in the closet. I think I saw a segment about a murderous fiend hiding in a hotel room closet on *Dateline* once, or maybe it was a trailer for a horror movie, or maybe it was someone making a joke about the least rational fear ever documented. It doesn't matter. If I don't die on the plane or on the unknown roads, if I'm not mortally humiliated by a tollbooth attendant or murdered by the stranger who keys me into my room, there's always the person in the closet waiting to strangle me.

And that's the easy stuff. I spend the bulk of my travel minutes fixating on how my loved ones are probably drawing their last breath back home. Before you include this on the list of irrational anxieties, I should mention that while my mother and I were in New York City shooting location scenes for *The Goodbye Girl*, my father died of a heart attack in Los Angeles. I was nine. Yes, it only happened that once but it was kind of a big once. If you run into me at some airport and catch me with a faraway look, it's a safe bet I'm contemplating whether Alice has been exposed to Ebola at the nature museum or Daniel just ordered an E. coli burrito at Señor Muncho. I've been told I'm a wonderful traveling companion.

The fears continue to mount. This being a convention, they'll probably make me wear a name tag. Sure, wearing a name tag doesn't trigger the same degree of apprehension as thoughts of my imminent demise or the death of all my loved ones, but I really do hate name tags. I prefer to decide who learns my name, and when. If I do manage to live long enough to arrive at the Radical Unschooling conference and apply my name tag, these will probably be the sorts of people who, at some point or other, expect a hug. I don't like hugging strangers and am pretty certain I'm bad at it.

After years of behavior modification, I've been told I flinch only slightly when touched by unfamiliar people. All in all, it's probably best to stay home and mine the upholstery, collecting change for some future toll-related trip.

And yet, these people might be on to something useful. Maybe we *should* be encouraging our children to be brave and individualistic learners, unbowed by traditional classroom roles or bedtimes, solving the problems of the world with unique minds covered by blissfully unbrushed hair. Maybe these folks will become my brethren, my Radical homeschooling tribe. Maybe we'll make Tibetan prayer flags together, the pigment from my newly tie-dyed hemp serape dripping down onto my Birkenstocks as I watch Alice head toward her fully actualized life—a life that will involve algebra but only if she really *wants* it to involve algebra. If these people are right, won't I feel foolish for having missed out because I was afraid of a hotel room closet? I booked my ticket.

Neither Alice nor Daniel would be joining me. Daniel had adult things to do that were neither joyful nor, I suspected, anywhere near self-actualizing, but had a pleasing habit of paying him. Alice couldn't come because she was taking an online class and had a midterm exam scheduled for that week. She needed to study hard for the exam, which she would take in our kitchen under the watchful gaze of a proctor whose job it was to make sure she abided by all the rules and experienced nothing approaching fun. I decided I wouldn't bring any of this up to my new theoretical friends, because it made our life appear less than blissful. Nor would I bring up the hotel room closet maniac, because it made me appear less than sane.

My unresolved concern now became: Was it weird to go to a

gathering of unschooling families without an actual family? For one thing, the hotel's big selling point was an all-season, indoor water park—a feature that doesn't excite most people over the age of fifteen. Would I be called upon to explain why I was there by myself? Would everyone decide I was peculiar and not talk to me? Maybe I could simply tell any curious parent that my daughter was with me, just off enjoying "the largest indoor water park in New England!" according to the brochure. Three solid days left to her own devices in a water park; was that Radical or just neglectful? Maybe I'd allow Imaginary Alice to watch hours of TV in the room while I was at the conference. She could order room service and play video games. Real Alice had a long, arduous week ahead of her, but Imaginary Alice was going to have a ball.

The flight to Boston was uneventful except the part when we flew through a storm large enough to merit its own name. We bounced around like a marble on a waterbed in the back of a garbage truck careening down a logging road. On the plus side, most of the people on the plane looked the way I always feel. Hard-core worriers like me enjoy vindication. Once we landed, the car trip was long, rainy and crammed with tollbooths, causing me to run out of change pretty quickly. I summoned my inner Sacajawea and discovered I was able to create change at any of the Dunkin' Donuts outlets located every hundred or so yards along the route. The tollbooth collectors couldn't criticize my lack of tender but would have been completely within their rights to complain that all my quarters were coated in some sort of red jelly.

Entering the hotel lobby, I immediately recognized the Radicals. They weren't hard to spot. Sure, it was off-season and the conference represented the majority of guests at the hotel, but had this been high season and the place swarming with indoor water park aficionados and a random smattering of tourists, I still would have been able to point out the Radical Unschoolers with confidence. Most of them sported a look best described as part dairy farmer, part Deadhead, part Renaissance Faire employee. Had I needed a way for someone to identify me among this group, I'd have said, "I'm the one with the shirt collar." The clerk at the front desk handed me a key card. I smiled wanly.

I stood at the door of my room, inhaled a deep, calming breath and swiped the card. The red light remained red. Nothing else happened.

Swipe.

Red.

Swipe.

Red.

Swipe.

Green! Red! Wait, red? Where did green go?

Swipe.

Red.

A family in bathing suits and flip-flops walked past me, I assumed toward the water park. The smallest child, who was no more than four, said casually to her parents, "I changed my mind. I'm going back to the room to watch TV." Without comment, her mother handed her a key card and the little girl went skipping back down the hallway. The rest of the family disappeared into the elevator. This, I assumed, was Radical Unschooling at its most basic. The child had a need. She expressed it. She was allowed to meet it. I toyed with being shocked that someone wearing what seemed to be a swim diaper was deemed old enough to have private me time in a hotel room. I pondered what sort of healthy limits these children had. I considered what my reaction to Alice would have been had she made the same request. My strongest emotion, however, was regret that I hadn't asked this child to help me get into my room.

Mercifully, a maid wandered by and was able to outwit my door. I dropped my luggage, checked the closets for the maniac and headed back out to scope out the water park. If my daughter was going to spend the next three days there, even if only in my fevered imagination, it had better be worth it. A twisty corridor and several muggy airlocks later, I was facing New England's largest indoor water park. To my Californian eyes, jaded by water parks that sprawl across entire zip codes, this was a water park scaled for a dollhouse. It was more of a water room. And it was incredibly humid, like standing in a chlorinated lung. There was no way Alice would spend the better part of a week in Chuck E. Cheese's steam room. I would account for her absence later, but first I needed to eat.

I passed through the main conference room where several families had gathered around tables strewn with noncompetitive games. Until that moment, I had never seen a Rubik's Cube printed in a mandala pattern; the little peace signs were a nice touch. I walked to the registration table and signed in. A tall, healthy woman welcomed me with a tall, healthy hug. She handed me a schedule and indicated the nearby table where I could make and decorate my name tag. There were colored pens and sequins. I was encouraged to "get my bling on." Some combination of being touched, furnished with a name tag, having my creativity challenged and hearing a grown woman use the word "bling" overrode my neuroses and for the first time that day I felt almost calm. When she asked where my family was, I didn't blink.

"I chose to come, they chose to stay home," I said blithely, and an instant later found myself thinking, *Well done, Quinn. Very unschoolish.* I was either instinctively aligning myself with their belief system or I was developing a flair for pathological lying. I sidled off to find food without getting my bling or my name tag on. One Caesar salad later, I retired to my room, or more accurately, my door. A half hour of swiping later, I managed to get inside. I called Daniel and Alice to say good night, to tell them I loved them and to make sure they hadn't died.

The next morning, the first item on my agenda was a panel discussion about "Unschooling as a Life Philosophy." Excellent. That would be one radical discussion. I entered the conference room just as the introductions were beginning. There were five women on the panel and between them they had fifteen children, three of whom were named after continents.

"Where's Pyramus?" a young voice commanded from somewhere in the room.

The panel discussion was just warming up when a little girl crossed to the stage risers and stood in front of her mother.

"Where's Pyramus?" the girl repeated. She was about six.

Her mother, who was chairing the session, stopped midsentence and said, "I don't know."

"But I need him," the little girl said flatly. The other panel members and the audience looked to her mother.

"Have you tried the room?"

"Yes."

"The water park?"

"Yes."

"Have you looked outside?"

"Yes."

Stumped, the mother simply stared at her child. I tried to put myself in her shoes and determined that no matter how evolved I became, at least two sentences ago I would have indicated to my daughter that I was in the middle of something. I might even have pointed out the twenty or so people in the room who had not gathered together this morning to wonder where Pyramus was. Finally, the girl declared, "Ionia needs you. I'll get her," and wandered off. The conversation about respecting our children's need to live authentic lives without judgment or labels continued. A preschool-aged child got down from her mother's lap, undressed completely and dashed out of the room. A minute or so later, her mother followed her.

"You just need to keep filling the emotional cup: your cup, their cup," one audience mother volunteered, watching in delight as her child nursed at her breast and wove his fingers through her long hair. "Take the five minutes to let them know you really hear them."

Guilt enveloped me like a hand-woven poncho. Even when I was supposed to be giving Alice my full attention, I was often answering a text message, flipping through mail, hustling a cat off the kitchen table. If anything, homeschooling had made things worse because on any given day there was at most ninety minutes when I was a "me" and not a "we." These multitasking moments were my own little rebellion against the adored yet relentless presence of my offspring. But how much was I missing? I have a few blood relatives who lived well into their nineties. If I take after them, I could have decades of "me time" after Alice leaves home. Would those years be spent in deep regret over the "*we* time" I carelessly threw away today? Every person in this room seemed to glow with delight over her children, no matter how many she had or how loudly they were screeching. There was a presumption of joy and curiosity in whatever each child was doing. At one point, the panel leader suggested we make every effort to learn about whatever our children found interesting, even if it was *Pokémon*. I was the only one who laughed. This might not have been a joke.

I sensed that none of these women had ever hidden in the laundry room to get away from her child. I could tell that none of them hated Candy Land. Not one single person at this entire conference had ever driven past the nearest public school after an especially long week and heard the low, dangerous inner voice say, "You know, we don't *have* to homeschool. Legally, they have to take her. I could just leave her here." I was a horrible teacher and a thoughtless mother. And Alice would never taste a really fresh egg.

I skipped the group lunch, partially out of sorrow for all that I hadn't provided my daughter and partially because I saw the daily schedule promised "Pizza 'n' Karaoke!" which combined two of my worst fears: mandatory public singing and the frivolous amputation of the word "and." I hid in the solarium for the lunch hour, making a meal out of saltines and a peppermint I found in my purse. Thus restored, I dashed off to another meeting about . . . well, frankly, I have no idea. My notes from the lecture read: *Strive for something unlike a results-based paradigm!!!* underlined three times. Forgive me for not being able to further elaborate but I got a little distracted when an energetic boy of about four raced into the conference as I was writing that note. Spying his mother in the front row, he flew into her lap, hoisted out a breast and nursed for a while. After a few minutes, either he was no longer comfortable or he wanted a better view of the podium, so he inched out of her lap and sidled into the seat next to hers. It was an effortless move, made even more impressive by the fact that at no point during the entire maneuver did he disconnect from his mother's nipple. I've been around the Internet once or twice and seen a few things I'd rather scrub from my memory, but until that moment, had you asked me if an average-sized human breast could stretch halfway across a folding chair, I would have winced and whispered, "God, no." Several minutes after this demonstration of human elasticity, I realized my focus was less than sharp. I decided to go outside, take in a little fresh air and get a sense of the general mood of the gathering, study the traditional barometer of the community's mind-set. In other words, it was time to read bumper stickers.

It is safe to say that Radicals have opinions, and many of these opinions fit on bumpers. Apparently, you couldn't come to this convention unless you believe in practicing random acts of kindness and/or thinking globally while acting locally. The rest of the bumper stickers fell into two categories: (1) *We are a gentle, enlightened, mildly smug people*, and (2) *Don't make me pull this car over.*

Here were some of the smug ones. First, the Nursers:

Love your baby. Nurse them.

Breast is best.

I make milk.

Breast-feeding mother in car.

That last one fascinated me. First, the odds were small there would be a breast-feeding *father* in the car. Second, was I to assume breast-feeding was going on at that exact moment? God knows I had just seen how a child could be buckled safely in the passenger seat and still belly up to the bar for lunch.

And then, of course, there were also the Unschoolers:

Live free, learn free . . . unschool!

Did you know kids don't have to go to school?

Play is the only way the highest intelligence of humankind can unfold.

I've seen the village and I don't want it raising my kids.

Leonardo da Vinci: Another homeschooled genius.

I toyed with finding the person who owned the last vehicle and pointing out that pretty much everyone was homeschooled during the early Renaissance, but I noted they also had a fair number of the more intimidating bumper stickers glued to their van so I decided to give them some space. For instance, they really didn't like fluoride. Or vaccinations. In fact, nearly all the bumpers evidenced some concern about vaccines, many of them providing a link to one website or another in a tiny font. In case you weren't concerned by the road risk of a mother tearing down the highway and simultaneously breast-feeding someone in the backseat, consider the car behind her, its driver searching for a pen, squinting at a bumper sticker several car lengths ahead and trying to transcribe a web address called www.mercuryisawfulandvaccinescauseautismanddonotevengetmestartedonteflon.org.

Back inside, the next panel I attended was titled "Single Parent Unschooling." This intrigued me, not because Daniel and I aren't doing well—he's lovely and I see no way I could upgrade—but because, to me, homeschooling implies having at least one parent around to monitor all the learning tasks, the administrative tasks and the general, sort-of-improving tasks. It's hard to hold a full-time job besides parenting if you're never actually *not* parenting. I know one single woman whose teenage daughter homeschools at her computer in the kitchen while Mom works at an office downtown. The mother randomly Skypes her daughter during the day to make sure she's doing her schoolwork and not cutting her own bangs, getting pregnant or attempting other such unauthorized behavior. But the Skyping mom was of the online charter homeschool variety. How would an unschooling parent do it? Would she check in during the day to make sure her children were still delighted? I needed to understand how this worked.

I was the only person to show up for this panel. Even the woman who was scheduled to chair the discussion didn't show up until a few minutes later and seemed surprised to see me. "I figured no one was coming," she said. "But now you're here."

She wasn't terribly excited to talk to just one person and I was politely horrified to be the one person she felt compelled to talk to. Being the only audience member at a seminar is like being the target for an unwanted hug from which you cannot escape. We stared at each other for about a minute. "So." She finally sighed. "How long have you been a single mother?" I paused to consider how to answer this, but was stumped; having lied once the previous day, I had used up my creativity for the fiscal quarter.

"Actually," I whispered, "my daughter's father and I are together."

She seemed a little confused as to why I was there. So was I. I nearly blurted out how Daniel wouldn't let me raise chickens and this might lead to a breakup in the years to come, but the moment passed. Eventually, she began telling me how she unschooled as a single parent. During the week, she worked in another town while her son stayed with her sister, who unschooled her own children. She felt so deeply that this was the best possible way to be educated—in fact, to live—that she gave up five-sevenths of her time with him to make it work. I sat there in quiet awe of her conviction, this polar opposite of my self-doubting lurch through life. She was, in a word, Radical. But I considered the availability of her sister to execute this grand plan. I tried to imagine if an unschooled education was even possible with a parent who was truly alone at the helm, a single parent who had a full-time office job and no one to carry the load at home.

The panel was supposed to last about an hour, but what with my being the only person there and actually having a better half and all, we sort of ran out of things to say after about fifteen minutes. So when she suggested we end early, I eagerly agreed. I walked down the hallway, past a group of parents who were watching their children play *Guitar Hero*. I overheard one of the mothers say to her friends, "The best thing an unschooler can be is a trust-funder. Then, they and their kids can simply do whatever they want." After just learning about a Radical who boarded her child out every week with a relative so he could unschool while she paid the bills, it was hard to argue with that. Then again, she also might have said, "The best thing an unschooling family can have is a wish-granting genie. And a flying horse. And a wizard who will do your taxes and remember where the girl's retainer is," but I think that applies to any school situation. Hell, any *life* situation.

Maybe Gatto is right. Maybe school is stupid, soul crushing and irrelevant. But what if these traits are not liabilities of modern education, but features? How many of us are continually delighted by our work? I've spent my life around actors, some of whom were quite successful. A successful actor is well paid and is given the opportunity to do what he has dreamt of doing his entire life. He should be the most joyful person in the world. And yet most are happy to tell you their job is often boring and hardly wonderful. Maybe school is designed to acclimate humans to enduring long stretches of tedium.

It started to occur to me that whatever you think education should be is probably analogous to what you think life should be. People who prefer structure and order will thrive in an educational experience that is structured and ordered. Homeschoolers in this group will probably like an online charter approach. If you think life should center on God, you're probably going to want your children's education to center there as well. Radical Unschoolers see the ideal life as a being filled with unbridled enthusiasm, inspiration and discovery but few rules, so they approach their children's education with a heady balance of anarchy and delight. Is any one of these better than the others? Do any of them sound like my family?

As the afternoon wore on, I needed to clear my head. Luckily, a family yoga class was just starting in a breakout room. About eight families were getting warmed up; parents and children ranging in age from two to ten were strewn about the floor on mats. Everyone was working on downward-facing dog, with the exception of the youngest practitioner, a two-year-old girl who was trying to get the attention of a slightly older girl from another family. She strutted up to her new friend.

"My name is Indigo and I have a bagina!" she shrieked. She took off her pants.

I recognized this pixie as the fleeing nudist from the morning session.

"I said my name is Indigo and I have a bagina!"

She did a saucy cakewalk around the other girl. Her mother finished her pose and, smiling fondly, came over to sit next to her dancing, shrieking offspring. The other girl, who was about four, assumed a blasé manner I'm not sure I could have mustered had someone naked from the waist down insisted on being my friend with similar gusto.

"I'm Dora the Explorer and you can be my doggy!" Indigo bellowed at her.

The older girl pulled a wooden toy from her mother's tote bag and began to play with it. Indigo grabbed at the toy with covetous abandon. The older girl snarled loudly and punched Indigo in the sternum. Indigo shrieked back and whomped her upside the head with the toy. All the yogistas made a big show of continuing their poses, as if there was nothing better for a calming meditation than enraged children being authentic in full voice at close range. Indigo's mother gently took her daughter's hand, gazed deeply into her eyes and spoke calming words in a voice only they could hear. Indigo promptly hoiked out her mother's breast and nursed for a few minutes while Mom continued to hum softly and stroke her curls. In five minutes, Indigo was curled up in a contented torpor, quite happy to leave the other little girl alone and let her mother try tree pose. Everyone felt heard. Everyone felt stretched. I felt like a jerk for all those times I fled a public event because my two-year-old daughter was behaving like a glue-sniffing howler monkey when all she needed was for me to be just a little more patient and loving.

I shut my eyes to commune with the general good vibe of limbs being flexed and needs being met.

"I'm Indigo and I have a bagina! You should get up now!"

Indigo was back stalking her new friend; this time poking was involved. The other girl worked hard to ignore her. Then Indigo picked up the wooden toy and flung it at the teacher. I waited for her mother to figure out that Indigo was perhaps not in the mood for yoga. Instead, a diversionary breast was once again cantilevered out for service. This was enlightening, but not in the way I needed right now. I grabbed my towel and headed back to my room for a restful quarter hour of door stabbing. Finally inside, I called Daniel and Alice to tell them I loved them and to confirm that they hadn't died.

In the restaurant that night, I contemplated this new tribe I was test-driving. That morning, one of the speakers had told us that human beings come from one of two places: fear or love. If those were the only sources of human motivation, I knew where I got my mail. But in my case, I swear fear and love are joined at the hip: I *love* you so deeply that I *fear* all the possible things that might happen to you. Did I tell you about the maniac in the closet? It's safe to say that I am not one of those people inclined to experience life's grand adventure with open arms. As I watched the Radicals around me enjoying their dinners and each other's company, I began to understand that in the *fear* versus *love* tug-of-war, the word "love" could also be pronounced "faith." The people gathered here certainly had *faith* that a strong family—backed by a community of like-minded parents—could provide their children with sufficient volumes of love, motivation and confidence to guide them on the path to adulthood.

They had no fear that this might be the wrong strategy. In fact, the general attitude of these families was that the choice to live as Radical Unschoolers saved their children's lives. These parents would say, convincingly, that their children had only one chance to be children. The true act of faith, then, was to believe in their children's ability to discover what they needed and to seek those lessons on their own.

How was this any different from my original hopes for Alice a few months ago? How was this different from any good parent's desire to seek a healthy balance of accomplishment and happiness for their children? In fact, it wasn't. Yet even as I kneaded these ideas around in my head, I had no more faith today than I did that day when I sat on the laundry room floor and tried to inhale through a bag. I couldn't deny these kids seemed happy. For the most part, they seemed very happy. Heck, if I ever get to do things my own way all the time, I'll be very happy, too. So what was my problem?

My nachos and Syrah arrived, a dinner choice that said to the world: *Right now I don't have to model good habits to anyone*. The waiter asked if everything was all right. I had ample portions of both melted cheese and wine, so I assured him everything was perfect and went back to my reflections. What if I took the easy route—the path of least resistance, the option that promised the least friction and the most immediate pleasure for everyone, the educational equivalent of having nachos and wine for dinner—and let Alice unschool herself? What if we committed to this and it came out badly? That would be it. You get one chance to look at the menu options for childhood. Then you pick. There'd be no complaining to the waiter or reordering another childhood. I was the waiter. I was the kitchen. If this meal we call her childhood comes out wrong, it's wrong forever.

And even if the education part worked itself out, what about social behaviors? Could I make the argument that meaningless academic activities weren't worthy of her but meaningless social activities were critical? I always say "please" and "thank you," but when she was little, I tried to have Alice nearby every time I thanked someone, hoping it would sink in. *This is what we do; we are grateful when people are kind to us.* It didn't stick in her behavior until I'd spent six months being the Politeness Police, nagging her without cessation. Now, it's a habit. I don't remember the last time I had to remind her to say either "please" or "thank you." But if I had waited until etiquette interested her or until she was summoned to the Court of St. James, a lot of people who did nice things for her would have gone unrecognized. Was I prepared to take a "wait and see" attitude on everything?

In ancient times, behaving in a way that was acceptable to your tribe was a matter of life or death, sometimes literally. The occasional child who ate the red mushrooms or ignored the "don't-tease-the-bear-with-her-cubs" rule gave everyone else in the clan a revelatory few minutes as the consequences played out. Nowadays, tribal rules are more about quality of life than quantity. If you don't remember to wash your hands after visiting the toilet no one will eat you, although I reserve the right to shudder. But if we choose to adopt only those behaviors and learn only those lessons of our own self-defined tribe, we're going to have fewer places upon which to find common ground.

The Radical Unschoolers, I thought as I reached for a chip loaded with hot cheddar, were certainly right about one element of basic human nature: Education is best soaked up, not crammed in. Treating children as if they are livestock waiting to be told what to do and how to do it diminishes everyone involved. Every young person deserves the time and encouragement to discover his or her own gifts. But for every person trying to get their needs met by, say, making a friend or sharing an insight, there is another person perfectly happy being left alone and not hearing anyone scream about her genitals.

My nachos were a distant memory. I glanced at my phone; my flight was in six hours. I could start fretting about crashing shortly. I called Daniel with my arrival time and my love, and to make sure he hadn't died. I reminded myself to fill up with toll quarters. But first I had to have someone let me into my room, pack my bag and make one final check of the closet.

Le Math

* * *

Alice could have studied Spanish, the language so endemic to the city in which we live that its name is actually *Spanish.*

Alice could have learned Chinese, which, considering the amount of America's debt they own, might prove beneficial in the long run. She'd be able to renegotiate our mortgage.

Alice could have learned Armenian or Russian, and we would finally know what the grandmothers hiss when they cut in front of us at the farmers' market.

But we chose instead that Alice learn French. We assumed it would come in handy for her career. Her career in the diplomatic corps. Her career in the diplomatic corps circa 1955.

When Alice spent a year in the French-immersion school, my hope was that since I had studied French in high school I'd be able to help her with her homework. I had fond, dewy hopes of the two of us wandering down some street in our neighborhood, chattering away about *pain* and *lait* and *fenêtres*. The fact that every street in our neighborhood had a Spanish name didn't diminish my fantasy. What did diminish my fantasy was the fact that within two weeks of her starting French school, she was correcting my pronunciation. By the end of the first month my accent made her flinch. She wasn't just learning to speak French; she was learning to *be* French. Our bonding experience would come not in mastering an elegant Old World language together but in the gently scornful laughter my attempts to sing "Frère Jacques" would provoke.

The school didn't turn out to be the great saving of Alice's education but she continued to like the language and I continued to take some pleasure in being gently mocked by a tiny, on-site Francophile. We decided to continue her French studies in a casual way but for reasons already explained regarding my accent, we needed to find a French tutor. I handled this the way I handle many things in my life: I complained to everyone within earshot about how I needed to find Alice a French tutor or else bad things would happen—in this case, the bad thing being a tragic cross-contamination of Alice's accent with mine. Eventually, someone told me about a mother at her kid's preschool who was born in Paris and interested in tutoring.

"Merci!" I shouted in delight, causing Alice to grimace her perfect Gallic grimace and suggest *she* be the one to call the tutor.

Thankfully, the tutor spoke fluent English, so it worked out perfectly. Madame Rose is a delightful woman with a wildly adorable five-year-old daughter Louna; both of them qualify as the most Gallic-looking females since Audrey Tautou. If you were observing North America from a low-orbit spy satellite, you would say something like "Oh, look! The Hollywood sign! . . . And two French people!" One afternoon a week, Alice and Madame Rose would study French for an hour. Then Alice and Louna would trot out to Madame Rose's charmingly rustic yard and play in a sprightly yet civilized way while chatting in French. During this time, I would go off and do errands *by myself*—an activity I had taken for granted back before we homeschooled.

I certainly didn't take my freedom for granted anymore. On the first day of French maintenance, I did three errands in ninety minutes and had enough time left to knock back a twenty-ounce tea, or as I now refer to it: Quinn's Cup of Personality. When I picked Alice up that first afternoon, she hugged me in delight. I might not be able to take her to France but I could bring her to French people, and we'd all benefit. My, what a great mother I am. Now if someone could just tell me the secret of how Frenchwomen have such lovely, shiny hair.

"Do you know how to make crêpes?"

A month had gone by and we were driving home from Madame Rose's. It should be noted Alice pronounced "crêpes" correctly. You could practically hear that little beret over the first *e*.

I answered, "If by crêpes you mean thin, watery pancakes, I suppose I could do that."

She snorted at my ignorance. It seems Madame Rose had whipped up an order of crêpes that afternoon as the girls' afternoon snack. Madame Rose added Nutella to some, sweet butter to the rest. Crêpes were, without question, the most *incroyable* afternoon snack. *Ever.* Most of our afternoon snacks involved me saying, "I think the apples are washed," or "Are your hands broken? Make *yourself* egg salad," neither of which are crêpes slathered in Nutella.

America: 0, France: 1.

(When you consider that Madame eats crêpes filled with Nutella and still fits into tiny, tiny pants, it's more like America: 0, France: 6.)

Later that week, Alice was watching a French DVD of *High School Musical* and complaining, "Why are they calling golf shoes *Les chasseurs des golf*? That's not right, it's [something said quickly and confidently in French]." I glanced at the box.

"It wasn't dubbed for France," I explained, reading the label. "It was dubbed for Quebec."

"Oh, *Quebec*, that explains everything" she said dismissively, waving her hand. I noticed she was now pronouncing "Everything" as "Everyzing," the way the French do. I considered tucking a pack of Gauloises and a dog-eared paperback of *L'Etranger* in her Christmas stocking. The next week, she came home from Chez Rose aglow. Madame had steamed artichokes and taught Alice had to make vinaigrette, which they served as a dipping sauce for the steamed artichokes. Had I ever heard of this ambrosia?

"Yes, Alice, I have. In fact, I made you an artichoke last summer, which you declared to be a furry claw, spiky and impossible to eat. And vinaigrette is the same stuff your father and I put on our salads but which you turn up your nose at in favor of that bottled fluorescent-orange stuff."

Alice suggested that perhaps Madame Rose could show *me* how she makes artichokes and vinaigrette. But she then reconsidered, as it might be too complicated for me to learn. I think that was also the day Alice asked me to rent *The Umbrellas of Cherbourg*, which I remembered as being a sweet musical, forgetting it's a sweet musical that romanticizes unplanned teen pregnancy. When we first suggested homeschooling, some people hinted that this plan might indicate a megalomaniacal need to force Alice to grow up exactly like us. Not two months into our adventure, Alice, having considered us closely, was allying herself with the influential kid most unlike her parents. This is a common rite of passage for most children her age—but in this case, the influential kid was an entire country. I was actually fine with this, because while France has nuclear weapons and the ability to declare teal batwing-sleeved pullovers the must-have fashion item for fall, it's still far less threatening than some sixth-grade girls I've known.

And then France started coming places with us. We'd be at the dry cleaners, or walking the dog, or in line at the deli, and Alice—sensing a person within earshot—would switch to French and assume the role of an exchange student. This made me nervous, but not for the reason you might think; I could follow what she said pretty easily. Her French was clear, her vocabulary wasn't complicated and nearly every conversation was in some way related to how she was feeling a touch peckish.

"I have hunger," she would declare in French, in an accent even a Parisian might grudgingly accept, *"and I would like to eat a sandwich or maybe to be given a piece of ham to walk with."*

I would whisper frantically to her in English, usually something along the lines of "I know you want to eat. You *always* want to eat. Hush!" What made me nervous was how she was drawing attention to us. Don't forget, we'd be running these errands in the middle of the day, when other children her age were in school. I kept expecting a firm hand to clamp down on my shoulder; I would turn to discover a large, ruddy-faced man with a handlebar mustache glaring at me, his navy blue cap emblazoned with the words "Truant Officer." Ignoring my pathetic excuses regarding our homeschool experiment, he would throw me in the paddy wagon and cart Alice off to the nearest public school where she'd be forced to eat Limburger cheese and drink castor oil.

(My understanding of the legal protocols associated with compulsory school attendance begins and ends with *The Little Rascals*.)

In another version of this daydream, the child's insistence on speaking French drew the attention of the French ambassador as well as the truant officer. Both men would glare down at me from a great height. The ambassador would have a pencil-thin mustache and a monocle. Eventually, they'd take Alice to France and give her a piece of ham to walk with.

As it turned out, my public parental inadequacy would come not from France but from farther east. One fall afternoon, Alice and I were in our local grocery store. As was her custom, Alice was pleading in an eloquent and continental manner for some sort of confection. This wasn't hard as the entire aisle was filled with swollen bags of fun-sized saturated-fat morsels. I looked down the aisle to the endcap display where two-pound bags of Milky Ways were interspersed with orange plastic spoons and odd-shaped cutting utensils. Something dawned on me—something disquieting and powerful. I spun around. Adorning the adjacent aisle were dozens of plastic pumpkins. Overhead, an endless string of cardboard harvest moons swayed in the air-conditioned breeze. My heart raced.

"Alice," I said loud enough to interrupt her Proustian reverie on Hostess products. "What day is today?"

She sighed; even her sigh had a French accent. *"It is the twenty and six of the month of October,"* she informed me.

The twenty-sixth? How was this possible? What happened to October? This was the month I was going to be like those mothers who blog about all their fall-flavored activities and seasonal home embellishments. Damn it! We were going to write harvest poems, plant a winter garden and braid corn or something. Even those parents who believe Halloween is a dark satanic ritual don't actually *forget* it.

Augh! Alice's costume! I hadn't gotten her a costume!

In my defense, Alice began ruminating on her Halloween costume sometime in January. It was the only conversational topic I'd successfully managed to tune out. In an instant of panic, it occurred to me that she probably assumed we hadn't gotten her costume yet because I was waiting for her to come up with the Best Idea Ever. Her ideas tended to get more elaborate and expensive as the months progressed. Sequins were a running motif. Also, animal costars. And prosthetics. And pyro. Playing back her most recent Halloween monologue in my head, I queasily realized that Alice had mentioned she might go as Boadicea and could I please gather a few thousand Celts to mass behind her? I needed to pull out some high-level parenting skills this very instant or I'd soon be hiring extras.

I feigned excitement and bounced around a bit in the aisle. "Honey, listen. After we drop off the groceries at home, we're . . . going . . ."

Think.

"To . . ."

Think.

She waited expectantly, as did I. My brain raced. We needed a place with fancy outfits, a place with sparkly outfits for small girls, a place where I could eat something because my blood sugar was low and a eating a two-pound bag of fun-sized Milky Ways right here in the store would seem like a bad idea later.

I had a thought!

"Little India!"

"What?"

What?

"Yes," I said eagerly, grabbing her shoulder and gazing deeply into her eyes. "We're going to Little India to get some lunch and to get you a proper Indian outfit for Halloween. You'll be a . . . Bollywood dancer!"

We stood in thought. An elderly couple passed us in the aisle. I barely dared to breathe, because if this didn't enthrall her, my only other option was to dress her in a T-shirt and pajama bottoms; this year she'd go trick-or-treating as the mother of a homeschooler. Several seconds passed. Watching an opinion form in her head, I could feel my arteries constrict. In a moment of desperate inspiration, I whispered, "You realize this will involve eyeliner."

It took us about an hour to get to Little India, a trip that usually causes me to whine and muse aloud, *how much do I want great Indian food, really?* But on this day I was focused and determined. Mothers who forget major holidays get no pity from anyone. Alice hummed a little Piaf in the backseat while we located a restaurant we had patronized before. We ate a quick meal of delicious things in various shades of taupe, khaki and ecru, picked up some pastries for later and then set off to browse the Indian boutiques that line Artesia Boulevard. After several stores and several dozen outfits, Alice settled on one especially sparkly ensemble. From across the room, the proprietress saw me flip the price tag and wince. Eighty dollars. Instantly she was at my side, which was impressive seeing as she was four foot six and about 270 years old.

"You want it?" she whispered.

"It's a little more than I planned to spend," I whispered back. She grabbed my arm firmly. She weighed about fifty-five pounds, all tendon.

"What do you want to pay?" she exhaled.

How much did I want to pay? I wanted to pay nothing. I wanted her to give it to me. But something told me this wasn't the Indian Clothing Store Comedy Hour. I was supposed to come back with a number, and then she'd counter with a number, and at some point before I died and she ate my heart to maintain her immortality, we'd agree on a price. It was bargaining time. Once again, I was confronting something I was patently unqualified to do, something I couldn't subcontract to Madame Rose. I was negotiating.

I stalled.

"How much does one usually pay for something like this?" I murmured. I have no idea why we were murmuring. Aside from Alice, who was trying on toe rings, we were alone in the store. Perhaps one of the gods in the shrine by the front door was offended by people who speak loudly and can't negotiate.

The woman smiled. Or winced in pain. It was hard to say. "What *will* you pay?" she barked.

All I wanted to do was break down sobbing and tell this powerful ageless rani, "Listen. I can't speak French, I can't remember major holidays, I have no idea where I put the seeds we were going to use in the winter vegetable garden, this is the first time this week I've put on socks and I can't negotiate! I'm trying my best to educate and raise my child without actually doing her permanent harm. So for the love of yogurt-based drinks, *tell me how much I'm supposed to pay for this outfit*!"

I didn't do that. I breathed in and collected my thoughts . . . No one knows and no one cares. Alice doesn't know I almost forgot Halloween. The people who see Alice with me in the middle of the day neither know nor care why she's not in school. And this tiny woman doesn't know I can't negotiate and that she terrifies me. Just exhale and act as if you know what you're doing.

"I'll give you twenty," I stated using as flat a voice as I could muster.

We settled at twenty-eight dollars, with toe rings and a headpiece thrown in. Considering this was the first clothing I had bought my daughter since June, I could live with that. I went to the nearest grocery store, got Alice her own vial of eyeliner and declared Halloween done. On the way home, my only parenting job was to dissuade Alice from flicking her shiny new shawl at me while I drove.

When we got back, I decided that since it was now three o'clock we should actually do some educating before the autumn sun dropped over the hill. I dragged out her math book and noted we were still in probabilities. I smiled inwardly. We were good at this.

A wheel with a spinner and two colors had a 50 percent likelihood of landing on your color of choice. Three colors, 33 percent. Four colors, 25 percent. And so on. The day before, the math book had added a second wheel with two colors, but within a few minutes we calculated the odds of the same color landing on both cards. I was exultant and exhausted; all hail the conquering heroes of spinners. Alice turned the page and the cards developed three colors each; I started to worry a cuticle. Alice flew through it like a champ. I took a few minutes longer. Now she opened the book and we were assaulted with today's work: one spinner of two colors and one of three. There must have been a printing error. I flipped the pages around a bit, vamping, but no, this was neither a mistake nor a joke. Alice and I were actually meant to work this obscenity. I pointed at the problem and said to Alice, "So, um . . . you understand this, right?" There was no way she didn't hear my worried tone.

She looked at the book for a long moment and slowly offered, "I think so."

My newfound inner problem-solver piped up. "She understands it," I told myself. "No worries. I'll get the answer key from the answer-key hiding place. She can do her problems while I eat Indian pastries, and then I'll check them the easy way. If she's right, I move on. If she's wrong, I hand her to Daniel when he gets home and he figures out this multiple-spinner hell. No one knows I'm a math moron and everyone wins!"

Another voice in my head spoke up and said, "Quinn, this is where faking it stops. For her sake and yours, you must learn how to do this. Tell her you don't understand it. Send her off to read, and work these problems yourself until you can do them and explain them. You'll model good behavior about what to do when confronted with something you neither like nor understand. It's not as if her math is going to get easier. You might as well get used to having to do the homework with her. And stop nibbling at the pastries; they're for people who understand multiple-spinner probability."

I hate that voice.

It took me an hour, and several YouTube videos geared toward math students born after 2000, but I conquered her homework. I did it with all the grace of a mouth full of Novocain drinking a milkshake, but I did it. I had bested a level of my own inadequacy, and together we would bask in the good behavior I was modeling. I pranced into Alice's room to show off my accomplishment. She smiled at me kindly and said, "I actually figured it out and finished it about forty-five minutes ago. But good for you! Anything else? I'm reading now."

I backed out of her room. "Well, *merde*," I said to the empty hallway.

At least I had taught *myself* how to do it, right? That would hold me through Easter at the earliest, right? Wrong. I was now learning the Second Rule of Homeschooling: The curriculum can fly by faster than you expect. By December, Alice's math homework was unknowable and alarming all over again—a hissing, feral swarm of angles and exponents. Even the videos were discouraging. I soon discovered that if the instructor called a number an "integer," I might as well just stop right there and watch dust bunnies drift across the office floor for all the good it was going to do me. Sure, Daniel could teach Alice math, but she already knew that her father could drive a stick shift and I couldn't; her father could put up a tent and I couldn't; her father could stop the toilet from running all night and I couldn't. Soon enough, it would be reasonable for her to start thinking women were good for little more than light housework and breeding. I think of myself as a feminist and an indifferent housekeeper, so it behooved me to provide her with a strong, competent female role model that could wrestle math to the ground and dominate it. Which is why I hired Miss Stephanie.

(I might be lousy at numbers, but I knew that between math and French, I had just subcontracted out 40 percent of Alice's so-called homeschool education.)

Miss Stephanie had enviably bouncy curls and the kind of fundamental good cheer that led her to open a workbook and say: "Yay! Rhomboids!" She was an excellent tutor, helping Alice through the uncharted wilderness of elementary school math. For the last ten minutes of every session, after soberly telling Alice, "I really shouldn't be showing you this yet, but I think you'll get it," Miss Stephanie would introduce something new and mathematically chewy. These incursions into new math territory would have thrown me into a panic, but all Alice seemed to hear was that she was joining a very cool, very exclusive club. After one especially productive session, Alice flew into the house and chirped with delight, "Quadratic equations are actually pretty easy!" I beamed and reminded myself to offer Miss Stephanie one of my kidneys. But Alice wasn't finished. "Do you want me to teach you?"

Without thinking, I squealed in terror. Then, I whispered a soft, "Oh, no."

I had found my daughter a female role model who liked math and was good at it. Now I could give up the charade and return to my own default setting when confronted with the subject: soul-crushing anxiety and self-pity. But Alice wasn't having any of it. She grabbed my hand and led me to the kitchen table. She whisked out her math notebook and said sweetly, "I'm going to go through this once slowly for you. Then you're going to have to do it."

That day, I learned an important lesson about education: The teacher doesn't always have to be out in front. For instance, when it comes to my daughter and the Ironman triathlon that is math, the teacher can be the one coaching and shouting encouragement from the sidelines, as her father does; or the teacher can be Miss Stephanie, running alongside giving hints and tips. And then there's my kind of teaching, where I'm a block behind her, avoiding cracks in the sidewalk and whining every painful step of the way. But by watching me work through a problem and correcting my seemingly endless variety of mistakes, Alice gets better at her math, even if I don't. Every time she masters a concept, she has to teach me. And every time I behave like a caveman dropped in a lab at Caltech, I'm playing up my ignorance for her benefit. I like to think that. Still, I defy the average reader to look at this . . .

$$x=\frac{-b\pm\sqrt{b^2-4ac}}{2a}$$

. . . and not want to tug on your eyebrows until the visual fades.

Here's a hint: It fades faster if you have some fun-sized Milky Ways. I suggest the two-pound bag.

Veni, Vidi . . .

* * *

One popular form of homeschooling springs from the premise that the best educational methods flowered over two thousand years ago. Today, advocates describe this approach, called the *classical education model*, as providing a superior framework for modern education. In practice, the classical education model has three distinct stages: the Rules stage, the Logic stage and the Rhetoric stage.

The Rules stage occurs in the early years—during what we now call elementary school—as the child becomes an active participant in the acquisition of critical information and concepts. According to *The Well-Trained Mind: A Guide to Classical Education at Home*, by Susan Wise Bauer and Jessie Wise:

> During this period, education involves not self-expression and self-discovery, but rather the learning of facts, rules of phonics and spelling, rules of grammar, poems, the vocabulary of foreign languages, the stories of history and literature, descriptions of plants and animals and the human body, the facts of mathematics—the list goes on. This information makes up the "grammar," or the basic building blocks, for the second stage of education.

Translation: Because their brains are supple and pliant, students should expect lots and lots of memorizing. As the parent/teacher of a homeschooler, you will not have to do much memorizing, which is good because your brain has probably started its own stage: the Calcification stage. During the Rules stage, your child will learn a language, preferably one that is very dead. Latin and ancient Greek are traditional; so is Hebrew in certain cases. I suppose your child could learn Etruscan or Moabite if you can find someone qualified to teach it.

As the child approaches his early teens, what classical educators call the Logic stage, his brain evolves past the mere accumulation of data and begins to wrestle with abstract thinking:

> During these years, the student begins algebra and the study of logic, and begins to apply logic to all academic subjects. The logic of writing, for example, includes paragraph construction and learning to support a thesis; the logic of reading involves the criticism and analysis of texts, not simple absorption of information; the logic of history demands that the student find out why the War of 1812 was fought, rather than simply reading its

story; the logic of science requires that the child learn the scientific method.

For parents, this means your job just went from beaming in pride as your wee classicist recites the presidents in chronological order to snapping, "It's not the 'Boring War,' it's the Boer War! And I'm still waiting on your decently constructed paragraph about its causes."

As the student approaches high school, and despite relentless evidence to the contrary, his brain continues to mature. With this maturity comes the inclination to communicate with the rest of the world and to share the fruits of all the basic information and abstract reasoning he's been developing. This Rhetoric stage, as it is called, has its own unique characteristics:

> At this point, the high school student learns to write and speak with force and originality. The student of rhetoric applies the rules of logic learned in middle school to the foundational information learned in the early grades and expresses his conclusions in clear, forceful, elegant language . . .

Aside from the alarming presumption that fortifying the communications skills of an age group whose collective ambition is to get a tattoo might be a good idea, I found these concepts entirely thrilling. I imagined Alice and me memorizing important facts together, reading stories, maybe fashioning a toga or two to wear while we studied maps, sang national anthems (accompanied by our own lute), dug up original sources, diagrammed sentences and declined verbs. Alice would start begging for snacks using clear, forceful, original language. Seven years of education spread out ahead of us in orderly blocks complete with precise time requirements for each subject organized by day, week and semester. We would have specific goals to set and milestones to meet. And best of all, there was a book that explained everything.

Unfortunately for me, the book outlining the basic theory and practice of classical education runs more than seven hundred pages. The last book I read that was longer than four hundred pages had something to do with a feisty green-eyed heroine and Atlanta catching fire. After a few chapters, I understood the foundational basis of a classical education. After a few more chapters, I grew distracted and bored. A few chapters later I was not just distracted and bored but irritably distracted and clinically, relentlessly bored, at which point I decided I couldn't be expected to finish any book while the cats were so aromatic, so I washed them in the bathtub.

Two aggrieved yet clean cats, a scrubbed bathroom and a bunch of Band-Aids later, I returned to the kitchen to read about classical education but was quickly arrested by how tarnished the bottoms of the pans seemed hanging there on the rack.

After the pans were scrubbed and I reopened the book, I noticed the filthiness of the fireplace.

After the fireplace was spotless, I think anyone would have agreed the book—fascinating as it was—would have to wait until I checked the expiration dates on every bottle in the medicine cabinet.

In sum, I was seized by the cold realization that I lacked both the mental focus and intellectual rigor to even get through this book, much less practice its advice. If Bravo didn't air *The Real*

Housewives of Classical Education in the next two weeks, I was going to need another theory to pursue. Though I still believe the classical education model is incredibly appealing and probably works well in the production of excellent little Romans, I have been forced to conclude that it's not a suitable option for our family.

However, let me assure you, should I win the lottery tomorrow I'll hire a full-time classical education tutor for myself. I'll pretend I'm five years old and memorize all fifty states, the pantheon of Greek gods and a bunch of long, fancy poems.

Then I'll invade Gaul.

The Fourth R

* * *

As I pursued my investigation into the tribal customs of my fellow homeschoolers, I cast a wide net. Despite what Daniel might tell you, this was legitimate research. As with *field trip*, my definition of *research* is somewhat elastic. Quinn skipping across captioned cat websites, drifting through websites dedicated to selling European castles and charting the mating habits of celebrities all fall under the heading of *research*. Despite such side excursions, I soon stumbled across—and became fixated on—a subgenre within the homeschooling webisphere: Fundamentalist family blogs.

There are hundreds of such websites and browsing them was like eating sanctified potato chips. I simply couldn't stop. I imagine there must have been a founding father of Fundamentalist homeschool family bloggers, the guy who established the uniform style sheet for such things because with little variation, each features a family portrait with a half dozen or more neatly combed children and a biblical exhortation: *Train up a child in the way he should go: and when he is old, he will not depart from it* (Proverbs 22:6). Or: *Be not conformed to this world: but be ye transformed by the renewing of your mind, that ye may prove what is that good, and acceptable, and perfect, will of God* (Romans 12:2).

Without exception, these blog entries chronicle the daily joys and challenges of homeschooling, following the Lord and preparing food in bulk. For more hours than I am prepared to admit, I happily scrolled through the minutiae of Fundamentalist families' lives, obsessed by how alien these people seemed in comparison to everyone I know. I'm not a complete Jacuzzi-soaking, cappuccino-drinking West Coast cliché. I have friends who are politically conservative. I have family who are socially conservative. I have broken bread with evangelicals. But outside of these Fundamentalist homeschool family blogs, I had never encountered a single person who prays over whether to buy brown shoes or black, who travels five hundred miles to visit a creationist museum or whose engagement ring was placed on her finger by her father because the Bible frowns on couples touching during courtship.

Reading about their scripture-centric lives, unflagging faith and Campbell's soup–based casserole recipes made me say, "Ooh," in that mildly envious way. I had found yet another homeschooling community with strong convictions and once again, I heard the siren's call: "What if they're right and I'm wrong?" Their sublime self-confidence that they had found the only way to educate, to live and to choose shoe colors caused me to lie awake at night thinking about how nice it must be to *not* lie awake at night wishing you believed in something. Next thing I knew, I was sitting in the kitchen at four a.m. skimming website after website of smiling piety and limited wardrobe options.

The Fundamentalists aren't slapdash dressers. The boys all seemed to wear buttoned-up polo shirts that are easy to find in any big-box store. The girls are also all neatly dressed, but each family interprets the Book of Timothy's admonition that "women should adorn themselves in respectable apparel, with modesty and self-control" in its own fashion, wearing anything from knee-length skirts and arm-covering blouses to dresses that were last in style when buggies ruled the road. This wardrobe is not assembled by a spontaneous trip to the mall. No, this look requires work. It's an outer manifestation of their inner conviction. One night, while web surfing for new pockets of piety, I discovered a vein of even more distinctive Fundamentalist style. Here were families who found a whole new place to wear their righteousness: on their heads. Women of every generation were now wearing a modest kerchief during all waking hours because:

> Every woman who has her head uncovered while praying or prophesying disgraces her head, for she is one and the same as the woman whose head is shaved. Or if the woman be not covered, let her also be shorn: but if it be a shame for a woman to be shorn or shaven, let her be covered. —1 Corinthians 11:5–6

Fortunately, 1 Corinthians has no beef with digital photography or HTML, so page after page, hour after hour, I would gawk at the screen until Daniel would appear at my side and gently lead me away.

A few weeks after making this discovery, I was strolling through Target and noticed a woman wearing an ankle-length skirt, a long-sleeved blouse and what appeared to be a doily pinned to her head. Quickly scanning the aisle, I spotted five or six younger women, all equally ankle-lengthed, long-sleeved and head-covered. I was so excited I actually squeaked. Had I bumped into Brad and Angelina comparing prices on antifreeze, I would have shrugged it off as just another quirk of living in Los Angeles. But a covey of conservative Fundamentalists trying on pastel hoodies thrilled me to my core. As they walked toward the bath towels aisle, it occurred to me that I should spend some real time with Fundamentalist homeschoolers. I was feeling my usual fascinated tug toward people who had actual dogmas and beliefs. Also, it couldn't hurt to get to know Fundamentalists a little better because as a homeschooler, I was pretty much in their house now.

There is no typical homeschool family. There are families who move frequently for professional reasons or because a parent is in the military, so it's easier to provide a consistent education from home. There are families who don't have access to a good school, or who don't want to put their children on a bus before the sun comes up and get them home after it sets. There are families who have profoundly gifted children, families whose children have social or emotional complications and children whose physical disabilities are not easily accommodated in a typical school setting. And there is a family in Los Angeles whose child was homeschooled because she refused to capitulate to the demands of long division.

But if you tell people you homeschool, they automatically assume you are devoutly religious and socially conservative. This is not an unreasonable assumption. In a 1999 U.S. government survey that asked, "Why are you homeschooling?" 33 percent of the respondents checked "religious reasons," 14 percent checked "to develop character/morality" and 8 percent objected to what was being taught in the public school. There may be atheists who are sufficiently concerned about morality and wary of public education to consider homeschooling, but the majority of homeschool program publishers aren't targeting nonbelievers as a worthwhile market.

There are thousands of online vendors selling education material for homeschooling parents, but more than half of the offerings are geared toward conservative Christians. Visit any one of these publishers' websites and search the term "evolution." You will be presented with numerous options, most of which portray the face-off between Intelligent Design and evolution as a lopsided competition in which Intelligent Design possesses the brilliance and agility of the Harlem Globetrotters while evolution is the Washington Senators, trotted out sacrificially to demonstrate the superiority of the marquee brand. The largest homeschool education company lists 212 products in its Creation Science/Origins of Life category, most of which can be summed up by the phrase, "Darwin, what a tool."

In the comments section of one publisher's website, a parent wrote to say how she and her daughter found a particular Intelligent Design textbook illuminating, but expressed concern that "the present-day dinosaur sightings seemed a little far-fetched."

This was one of the more mainstream publishers. There are

homeschool textbooks that take the position that God was on the side of the South during the Civil War and that the Africans abducted into slavery were lucky because they were rescued from a heathen continent and delivered to this godly land. Even further out on the fringes are textbooks based on Kinism, a recent spur of the Christian Reconstructionist movement, which blends religious fundamentalism with a mystical faith in American exceptionalism. Kinists advocate, among other things, the return of antimiscegenation laws and the rejection of capitalism in favor of a "covenant-based" economy. Obviously, that's a very small percentage of the homeschooling population, but the fact remains that much of the material geared toward the homeschool community assumes the reader is socially conservative.

From the Fundamentalist perspective, the first priority of homeschooling is not giving our children the skills required to succeed in society but protecting our children from the corrupting influence of that society. That unwillingness to mingle was probably one reason why, despite all the homeschool textbooks edited for their beliefs, I'd never met one of these families socially. If you think of homeschooling as a big get-together, I hadn't yet met the hosts of the party.

This struck me as regrettable—so much so that the urge to attend a Fundamentalist homeschool conference landed on my head like a modest handkerchief and would not let go. And then, late one night, I discovered there was to be a conservative Christian homeschool convention the following week.

It was like the answer to a prayer.

Rhymes with Orange

* * *

The conference was in a small town 150 miles northeast of San Francisco. I couldn't drive because I had to be home the next day, so I was going to have to fly. Though San Francisco is only a forty-five-minute flight from L.A., that's another forty-five minutes spent in the air wishing someone would just hit me with a frying pan so I'd relax a little bit. That I'd have to rent a car once I got there and drive another three hours meant I couldn't invite my usual airline companions, Countess Valium or Lady Vodka Tonic. I'd be flying solo. In the next few months there was sure to be another Fundamentalist homeschool convention within driving distance of my home but I couldn't wait. I was on a mission. One might even say I had a calling.

Not only would I fly, I had to craft an ensemble that would

allow me to walk freely among them without being stoned, shunned or smote. I set about creating a look for Quinn the Homeschooling Fundamentalist.

Fortunately, I didn't have to rent anything. This assignment didn't require a giant panda costume or a loincloth and sequined tiara—but if I'd run into anyone who knew me, they would have been no less bewildered by the outfit I did end up wearing.

From the back of my closet I unearthed a below-the-knee skirt I'd bought three years before and worn once. I had bought it because I thought the skirt made the catalog model looked tall and slender. After having it tailored (which meant I couldn't return it), I came to realize what made the catalog model look tall and slender was that she was tall and slender. The skirt made me look twenty pounds heavier and depressed. Eastern Europe depressed. But I owned it, and it was certainly modest.

The top took a while to figure out because every shirt I owned that matched the skirt exposed my upper arms. I couldn't decide which was worse: promiscuous arms or clashing colors. A cardigan solved the problem nicely. I spent entirely too much time ruminating over whether flip-flops were modest or Jezebel-ish. As far as I could recall, the Bible never delved too deeply into matters of footwear, so I chose the flip-flops. At the last moment, I recklessly painted my toenails because, to the best of my admittedly limited knowledge, the Bible never specifically enjoined against it. I did, however, go with shell pink.

Fingers were another matter. I wondered if godly women wore fingernail polish. Looking at my own nails, I thought, *Crap, they're chipped already.* Since I suspected godly women didn't think things like *Crap, they're chipped already*, it seemed safer to take it off. Doing this, I noticed something even more troubling.

I called to Daniel in the other room, "You still have your wedding ring?"

Daniel was married at one point. Our commitment, though deep and enduring, is less formal; no civil or ecclesiastic authority was involved. No rings, either. Luckily, Daniel never throws anything away. Within minutes, I was winding tape around the inside of his old gold band so it would fit my finger. I could pretend-marry Daniel to fit in with the Fundamentalists but I couldn't pretend-dump him for the Radical Unschoolers. I'm romantic that way.

I then had another flash: a cross! My ensemble absolutely required a cross. My daughter had been given a beautiful antique crucifix by a loving friend that she didn't wear for fear of losing it, so of course it was now missing somewhere in the house. I raced to Target. A half hour later, I returned with foot powder, a chew toy for the dog and a fourteen-karat manifestation of divine love and sacrifice glistening modestly below my collarbone. My hairstyle was too short and my excited giggling a bit out of character, but in every other way I was a Fundamentalist homeschooling mom off to a convention of like-minded, well-saved souls.

There are more than three hundred homeschooling conventions in the United States every year. The largest of them welcomes thousands of visitors. This was not that convention. Four hours of flying and driving later, I found myself in the middle of a small hotel auditorium with about seventy other people. I was delighted to see that nearly all of them had gone with the shapeless skirt/loose blouse/flip-flops look. Many were also wearing an infant. A borrowed infant would have completed my camouflage, but I'll go only so far for verisimilitude. I drifted around the vendor tables, most of which took their design cues from a grade-school science fair. There would be a cardboard sign on an easel with the name of the vendor and pictures of smiling people enjoying whatever product was being hawked. Some of the edgier vendors had pictures of sad, nervous-looking people who apparently did not yet know about the product or its miraculous properties.

I have been to a few trade shows in my time and been accosted by a sales rep or two, but let me assure you, these Fundamentalist vendors—out of concern for my eternal soul or the lower-than-expected turnout—were exceptionally eager to close the deal. The woman at the first table was selling biblical stories for preschool- and kindergarten-age children. She possessed the ability to breathe while talking. This prevented me, or anyone, from interjecting, "It's been swell, but I need to visit the Hairy Esau candle maker now."

Expertly blocking my escape route, she held up yet another book and flipped randomly though its illustrations. "This," she said enthusiastically, "is a book of the Twenty-third Psalm, written from the perspective of the shepherd. See?" She pointed to a shepherd lying against a tree, his sheep lounging sheepily around him. "And this is the line illustrating 'He maketh me lie down in green pastures,' because, see, what I didn't know until I read this book was that shepherds have to make sheep lie down after they eat, otherwise they don't digest right and can explode."

We looked at the picture. I noticed the unexploded sheep. She pointed again.

"And that's like how God makes us lie down and rest for our own good sometimes. See?"

This was new. If we choose to ignore God's postprandial rest, we might explode. Like sheep. Until now, my biggest fear was the cramp I might get if I went swimming too soon after lunch. Now I had this to worry about. I toyed with my crucifix while she turned more pages and charged onward.

"And here is the verse 'Thou anointest my head with oil.'" She continued brightly, "And, see, the shepherd is putting oil on the sheep's head. I just learned recently that shepherds would anoint a sheep's head with oil so flies wouldn't get into its eyes and lay eggs. Because, see, if the fly's eggs hatch in the sheep's eyes, the sheep can go blind. And insane."

I was actually throbbing with questions but I was in their world now, where the Bible is meant to be taken quite literally. Best to smile politely and nod. Still, one question popped out of my mouth. "So," I began in a tone which I hoped sounded modest and credulous. "Without God's oil on us, we could go blind and insane?"

"Yes," she said soberly. "That happens all the time. Now," she continued, suddenly smiling again and not missing a beat. "How many would you like?"

The next booth had a banquet-sized table elbow-deep in pamphlets, folders and clipboards. Across the back curtain hung a banner that asked in bold, stern letters: "Who Will Decide What Your Children Believe?" As I approached, the two women running the booth jumped up and started talking to me very rapidly, both at the same time. I'll condense the next twelve minutes with this summary:

The United Nations has a treaty about the rights of children. If America ratifies this treaty, the United Nations will be able to come into your house and take your child. This has already happened in Europe. A child was taken in Europe! If this treaty passes, children could choose their own religion and could become witches. Witches! Also, they could be taken. And not just in Europe, but right here in America. Parents could no longer spank their children. The only thing between us and men in blue helmets knocking down our doors and arresting us mid-spank is a constitutional amendment protecting the rights of parents. Because of this very treaty, the Supreme Court had nearly taken away every parent's rights but, praise God, enough justices saw the light.

After a few more minutes of blue helmets, witches, spanking and more blue helmets I feigned a proper level of concern, grabbed one of each pamphlet and slid away before blurting out how they might want to lie down in green pastures before they exploded.

At the end of the first aisle, I found a booth with hundreds of books covering topics that ranged from preschool colors and shapes to high school physics. There was a long shelf of books just for parents, organized less by subject matter than size and shape. *How to Survive the End of the World as We Know It* was displayed next to *Cutting Your Family's Hair.* The science texts included *Swimming Creatures of the 5th Day*, *Flying Creatures of the 5th Day*, and *Land Animals of the 6th Day*. I didn't see a book titled *Geophysics of the 2nd Day*, but I'm sure it was there, assuming the second day and the third day came to some sort of agreement as to who owned what.

For Alice's age group, I could buy the entire Creation Science Club series. This is an anthology about a group of middle school students whose mission is to "collect scientific stones of truth so they can meet and defeat the giant—Evolution." I assumed these scientific stones of truth are less than six thousand years old. While I scanned the other titles for something to get Alice as a travel present, a young mother in the next row asked plaintively, "Do you have any faith-based geography books?" As the bookseller helped her locate one, I had to pause a moment to think what that might mean exactly. Eventually, I found *Herodotus for Children*, which seemed kind of constructive, so I purchased it in what I hoped was a modest way.

The next booth was devoted to the newest trend among Fundamentalist educators: the stay-at-home daughter. Apparently, after finishing homeschool, some daughters are choosing not to continue their formal education but instead remain at their mother's side to perfect the homemaking arts. I'm sure some percentage of Christian daughters have been doing this for centuries, perhaps just never defining it any more specifically than "waiting for Pastor Right." Today, these girls are a proud and well-organized demographic and, as such, deserve products geared specifically toward their needs. I flipped through a few of the books on display. There were chapters on stain removal, on creating a welcoming home, on preparing delicious and nutritious meals on a budget. It was deflating to realize how much my own family's quality of life might improve if I replaced myself with a Fundamentalist stay-at-home daughter. If nothing else, the stains would be gone and they'd know the joys of a well-crafted meatloaf. Something to discuss with Daniel when I got home. Also on display were numerous books about homesteading. I guess this made sense in the event your stay-at-home daughter was courted by a fur trapper. One chapter on dressing a deer was particularly thorough and included many instructive photographs.

Plastered everywhere were flyers announcing hourly screenings of the documentary film *Homeschool Dropouts*. Since I manage to quit nearly everything I start, this seemed like something I should see. The screenings took place in a darkened room that could seat about fifty people. There were four in attendance at my screening, all huddled in back near the door. The light switched off and the video started.

Homeschool Dropouts covers a very serious topic. I know this because everyone talking on camera looked very serious. Sadly, I have no idea what they were saying because something was wrong with the video player or the PA system so the audio sounded as if a sinus infection had ruptured our eardrums. One very serious man kept talking about what sounded like oranges. He jabbed the air with his index finger a lot so I knew he was pretty wound up about these oranges. But it couldn't be oranges, could it? I racked my brain for a controversial topic that sounded like oranges. Prayer in the schools? Evolution? Sex educators? United Nations? Then I remembered nothing in the English language rhymes with oranges. He may very well have been going on about citrus. Or oranges might be a metaphor. But for what? Did the others know what he was talking about? I looked around and noticed the other four audience members had left. It was just me and the guy running the video, and he didn't seem to notice, or care, that the sound was unintelligible and that we were alone in the room. Either the Rapture had just occurred or it was okay to leave.

Back in the auditorium, an exuberant woman in a pastel bridesmaid's dress was hawking a history program to a mother and her three preteen sons. The bridesmaid said to the boys, "I have a question for you. Was God lonely before he made the angels?"

The boys were neatly combed and wore pressed-to-a-crease polo shirts and khakis, but they were still boys. One stared meaningfully at the sky, another dug in his pockets and the third entertained himself by breathing through his mouth. The bridesmaid continued, "If a Jewish person were to come up to you, what would you tell them about God?"

The mouth-breather swallowed and said softly. "He's . . . nice?"

"Well, yes. He's nice. But what might you call him?"

The boys conferred. Mouth-breather, their appointed spokesman, said, "Um . . . God?"

Bridesmaid nodded enthusiastically. "Yes, God! Is there another name for God?"

The boy who had been digging into his pocket raised his hand.

Bridesmaid turned to him. "Yes? What's another name for God?"

The boy's hand stayed raised above his ear. "Do you know where the bathroom is?"

Bridesmaid held fast. She had a point to make, she was going to sell this family her history program, and these boys would participate in the Socratic learning process whether they wanted to or not. I empathized. One woman's catechism is another woman's long division with remainders. Bridesmaid finally got the boys to admit that sometimes God is God and sometimes he's Jesus Christ and sometimes he can also be . . .

"Be the . . . What? . . . The what? . . ."

The boys gazed longingly at the door.

"The Holy . . . What?"

One whispered, "The Holy Spirit?"

Bridesmaid and I both slumped in relief.

"Yes, the Holy Spirit! And this is why God is never lonely, because there is always three. And what do we call the three? The Tr- . . . trini- . . . trinit- . . ." she prompted.

My wedding ring might be borrowed from my divorced baby daddy and my crucifix spent time in a shopping bag with foot powder, but even I knew the word "Trinity." The boy who had been staring at the sky raised his hand. She beamed at him.

"Yes? The Trini . . . ?"

"I think I have to go to the bathroom, too."

I silently wished her luck and crossed to another display, where I stopped in delight. The booth tenders here were one extended family, all big-boned, blond and, even for this room, modestly clad. The girls wore ankle-length dresses and matching headscarves made from the same fabric. The men wore white dress shirts buttoned to the neck and full beards beneath a shaved upper lip. I had found Mennonites. I felt all warm and bubbly inside, like a birder who'd just caught a glimpse of an extremely rare woodpecker. Their book selection made the Creation Science Club seem racy by comparison. All the other booksellers I'd visited had at least one or two titles based on Greek and Roman texts. It would seem Fundamentalists have no problem with the standard-issue classics as long as any gods or goddesses illustrated therein are wearing vestments that look like housecoats. On the Mennonites' shelves, every book fell into the "We have many options: Old Testament or New Testament" category. Also, they were big on flash cards. A display board set up behind the main table featured two sample cards joined together to read *Everything Is . . .* and *. . . About God.* Even without seeing the other cards, I knew a frisky teenager could blend them together until the cows came home and still never come up with anything even remotely suggestive.

Directly across from the Mennonites was a booth for a Christian family camp. The literature promised to *Reach the lost. Equip believers. Restore His servants.* Also, *Paintball & Snow-tubing!* The winter youth retreat promised *Challenging Chapel Time.* My mind hovered over the "challenging" part; perhaps that's where paintball comes in. Next spring's family retreat had an especially somber tone. One of the promised speakers belonged to Voice of the Martyrs—which, until that moment, I would have assumed to be a Swedish death metal band. Reading further, I learned that family activities included *Underground Church, Land Survival and Land Navigation.* I was hoping for a trip to Europe next summer, but perhaps we should start hoarding canned foodstuffs instead. We should also remember to rest after we ate our foodstuffs to avoid exploding in the underground church

Speaking of foodstuffs, as with conventions everywhere, each booth had a bowl of candy strategically positioned to attract strollers-by. The Christian camp's candy bowl included those green, foil-wrapped chocolates with a layer of mint inside—the ones you see on your better class of motel pillow. I have a weakness for these mints, so I modestly plucked one out. Then, having not eaten since before I left Los Angeles that morning, I grabbed two more. Fundamentalist Quinn's guard must have been down just enough for Inappropriate Quinn to emerge. I smiled in a friendly thank-you sort of way and said to the guy at the table, "Forgive me, for I know not what I do." His horrified silence had its own cologne: brimstone. Apparently, a gold cross over her heart and an elbow-covering shirt won't absolve a short-haired, sugar-addicted harlot for making a crucifixion-themed wisecrack.

It was probably safe to say I needed a break. The food options in the concession area were limited: a doughy slice of pizza that resembled an oil-stained throw pillow or an immense chocolate chip cookie, either of which would have rendered me sleepy and peevish in thirty minutes. I ventured outside for some fresh air and the hope of a nearby salad. Crossing the parking lot, I studied the bumper stickers. There didn't appear to be a lot of Obama fans in the crowd, but there were quite a few bumpers that proclaimed *Sarah? You Betcha!* or *Don't blame me, I voted for the American.* A minivan declared *Rejecting socialism isn't racism. It's patriotism.* Another welcomed me to Obamastan. More than a few reminded me that from time to time the tree of liberty must be refreshed with the blood of patriots, and quite a few more wanted me to know that abortions stop a beating heart. One had a picture of a fetus with the words *Mommy, don't kill me!* scrawled in jagged letters across the bottom, possibly indicating how difficult it is for the prenatal to wield a pen. A majority of the rear windows declared proud allegiance to the National Rifle Association. I envisioned all those cold, dead, homeschooling hands.

* * *

Judging by the slogans, you'd think these folks were a rather bristly bunch. Yet I had chatted with quite a few women inside, and most of them were terribly sweet. One woman, upon hearing I had flown up for the day from L.A. and was going back again that night, impulsively grabbed my hand and said, "Honey, no! Stay at a hotel. Take a night off. Let your husband take care of the kids!" When I told her I couldn't justify the cost, she said sincerely, "Well, if we weren't building a new bedroom, I'd have you come and stay at my house tonight." And I believe she meant it. I reminded myself that one of these bumper-stickered vans might belong to that kind woman and instructed my tenacious inner voice not to judge but simply to observe and reflect. From the parking lot, I couldn't see a single restaurant in the vicinity, but the fresh air had a restorative effect. I decided to risk a slice from the conference concessionaire.

I did not judge. I observed and reflected. I observed that the pizza was greasy, weirdly resilient and cold. I reflected on what eating an oleaginous whitewall tire might do to my digestive tract. After a protracted exercise that involved much chewing and blotting, I stumbled back to the conference area, into a workshop that promised: "Steel in my backbone as a homeschool parent." The word "steel" reeks of fervor and certainty, which is another way of saying conviction; you didn't need to ask me twice. The speaker was a tiny blond woman who was filled with the Holy Spirit and righteous fury. She was dressed in a pink cotton dress appropriate to the climate—both spiritual and meteorological—but had I been appointed to choose her ensemble for the day, it would have involved mostly camo and Kevlar. The meat of her speech was that we Christians are at war, and the enemy is everywhere.

The media is the enemy. She had proof: "Sarah Jessica Parker ate a cupcake in front of the Magnolia Bakery on that horrible show and started this whole cupcake craze. That's how powerful they are!"

The enemy is also "any member of your family who doesn't agree with your decision to homeschool."

Furthermore, she added, "The pharaoh is after your seed!"

By this point, things were becoming less clear by the minute, at least to me. Did we need to fear ancient Egyptian royalty as well as the cable networks, the UN and oranges? To the people in the audience, however, it was becoming increasingly obvious that the enemy was everywhere, even in our own souls. Before coming onstage today, the Pink Warrior told us she fasted and prayed because, as she admitted from the podium, "I don't trust my own flesh and I don't trust my own self."

A flash of empathy here. Left alone in the house with a pie, I will eat the pie.

Loopy as it was at times, her lecture raised an important question: If you can't trust your own best instincts, what can you trust? According to the Pink Warrior, the only safe refuge was within the welcoming arms of the Bible. But that didn't mean you could just kick back and relax there. "The Bible is filled with words of war," she warned us. "If you want peace, you'll have to make war." The PowerPoint projection flipped from images of boxing gloves to lines of scripture:

> For the weapons of our warfare are not carnal, but mighty through God to the pulling down of strong holds.
>
> —2 Corinthians 10:4

Click.

> Fight the good fight of the faith. Take hold of the eternal life to which you were called when you made your good confession in the presence of many witnesses. —1 Timothy 6:12

Click.

> So Joshua smote all the country of the hills, and of the south, and of the vale, and of the springs, and all their kings: he left none remaining, but utterly destroyed all that breathed, as the LORD God of Israel commanded. —Joshua 10:40

She liked that last one especially, noting that as Christians, "We have to stop leaving our enemies breathing." I looked around at the roomful of people quietly listening and taking notes. I like breathing, and I was fairly sure I was the closest thing to an enemy in the room. I inched down lower in my seat.

As the conference wore on, I began to get the prickly sensation of being followed. The United Nations is taking our kids. The U.S. government is taking our rights. Swedish death metal bands are taking all the best names. One lecturer warned that our churches were losing their vigor. Another told us we had to build a wall around our families before we trained them up. This wall, however, was probably irrelevant because at least three books on sale at the conference lamented how too many homeschooled Christians left the church by adulthood.

Even here, there seemed to be some confusion. One book had this attrition at 67 percent, another at 71 percent and a third at 80 percent. Nor was there consensus about what "leaving the church" actually entailed. Did it mean drifting toward a less Fundamentalist congregation? Changing your name to Muhammad? Setting foot in Abercrombie & Fitch? Whichever exit one took, there was general agreement that an unsettling proportion of Christian homeschool graduates were taking up cupcakes instead of arms. We must try our best and pray for strength, the general feeling went, but it doesn't matter because we're losing and the game's almost over.

Which was remarkable because these people had won a great victory in the very recent past. They were the reason homeschooling even officially existed in the United States. In the early 1980s, a coalition of Christian conservatives started to lobby in each state for legislation that made homeschooling legal in all fifty states, and by the middle of the 1990s they had succeeded. Yet they still didn't believe they had separated far enough from the tainted society they feared and so eagerly rejected. To their thinking, Big Government was still trying to break up their families, popular culture still held their beliefs in contempt and a global conspiracy of atheists and fervent anti-Christians continued to thwart their mission to satisfy God's directives. By the end of my first day as a pretend Fundamentalist, I realized that these people—burdened by the weight of their convictions, not to mention their modest clothing—were even gloomier than I was. And while I only had a vague sense of unease, they had Revelations to back them up.

So the plan now was to separate even further from the century that had sprung up all around them like a flood. Of course, all the ankle-length skirts and books about homesteading and bread baking weren't going to change the fact that these people were sending their children into a future they didn't like or understand.

The last speaker of the day ended with a prayer for all of us to go out and "Raise our children up right, teach them not to be afraid to fight sin and corruption." I could go along with that. She and I might have had drastically different definitions of right, sin and corruption, but I lowered my head and closed my eyes along with everyone else in the room. And when the time came, I said, "Amen."

Go, Team

* * *

Shortly before we began homeschooling, Alice hinted, then asked and finally begged to be allowed to quit gymnastics. She'd spent five of her first eight years dusting rosin on her hands and she was understandably burned out, but she was also a child accustomed to at least two hours of physical exertion every day, so unless I was prepared to convert the couch into a pommel horse, we needed a new activity. Ideally, it would be a team sport, so that when strangers asked after her socialization I could sing out brightly, "She's on a *team sport*!" After a little online poking around, I discovered that water polo was the fourth most physically taxing group activity—and since the state no longer allowed children to dig mines, harvest cotton or build canals, my daughter was going to be a water-poloista. She'd have practice with all those lovely teammates every weekday so it would be perfect for her physical health. She'd be too exhausted at night to bounce on my couch so it was perfect for my mental health, not to mention our couch's longevity.

Another benefit of water polo was that I knew absolutely nothing about it. Being homeschooled meant Alice had very few activities in which I wasn't at least somewhat implicated. Her schoolhouse was *our* house. Her schedule was *our* schedule. Her hobbies were *our* hobbies—if for no other reason than they were spread all over *our* kitchen. We listened to the same music as we sat in the same room and ate the same pretzels. Alice deserved some activity in her life where my only participation was driving the car and writing the checks. She deserved Alice time. On a somewhat related note, I deserved icy drinks, possibly with salt encrusting the rim. This would be my reward for having to sit around a swimming pool five nights a week, rain or shine.

The first week was glorious. I was ignorant and she was exhausted. The minute we walked through the front door, she'd stagger into her room and collapse on her bed. I'd switch off her light, walk into the living room and have a legitimately adult conversation with Daniel. One of those nights I even had an icy drink with salt encrusting the rim. By the second week, she'd built up enough stamina to stay awake for an hour or so after getting home, during which time she wanted to discuss the nuances of water polo in great detail. Her new teammates were great! Funny! Wonderful! Except for the ones who were silly! Rude! Slow! I can't say it was compelling conversation, but no one could claim that my daughter wasn't socializing. But there went the hour of adult conversation. On the third week, everything went to hell. I, along with every other parent of an under-ten player, received an email from the team mother. She was moving back East. Who'd like to take over as team parent?

Whatever the email version of crickets is, she heard it. Her next email had a panicked tone. It wasn't really that bad, being team parent. Virtually no work at all. Lots of opportunities to bond with the other parents. Just a hint of paperwork followed by the lifelong admiration of children, peers and community. Oh, wouldn't someone become team parent? Please?

You see this one coming, right?

Actually, I was one of three suckers—uh, parents—who eventually stepped up, so the job was split into thirds. My specific assignment was deceptively simple. All I had to do was get people to pay the swimming pool fee, the athletic association fee and the "we-just-felt-like-adding-another-fee" fee. Each had to be paid to a different organization. One was collected monthly, one was semiannual and one followed the Phoenician lunar calendar. Someone was always in arrears. My public demeanor changed from blissful indifference—sitting idly in the stands flipping through a magazine—to behaving like the poolside button man for the water polo Mafia. I'd lurk up behind a late-paying parent and murmur in a flat, ominous tone, "*Jackson seems to love water polo. Be a pity if we had to pull him out of the pool because his fees aren't paid.*" And not only was I now the pool mobster, I was also the pool FBI. I was getting dirt on every player because, as I soon discovered, there's nothing like being a week behind on pool fees to make a parent nervously start spilling the beans about another family's athletic indiscretions. Gavin kicked his teammates. Leila tried to kiss the under-twelve boys. Branford was a crybaby.

Against my will, I began paying closer attention to Alice's dissertations during the drive home from the pool. Like Alice, I was now analyzing her teammates' behavior for useful social context. Unlike Alice, I wasn't actually enjoying it. Each time she'd relate some infraction committed against her during practice, my mouth would spew the appropriate lecture about learning to work within a team while my brain hissed, *Of course it would be Dalton and Jemma ganging up on her. Everyone says their mother's been checked out since her husband's affair.* And the next night, there I'd be poolside, my previous apathy jettisoned like so many spent limes.

Months passed. Alice continued to attend practice five nights a week, but was less captivated by water polo than I had hoped. Trips home were spent musing aloud about how nice it would be to not get kicked in the ribs so often or how it would feel to not have scorched hair and smell like chlorine all the time. But, I'd remind her, she was learning how to be a *team player*. Being a team player means working together with someone whose head you would like to push under the water and *could* push under the water but *don't* push under the water. It also means learning how to take an occasional kick to the ribs. Of course, I wasn't a team player. I was becoming resentful. The fee collections never ended and someone was always ignoring my emails, phone messages and frantic waving. At one point, I toyed with simply shouting across the pool how much a certain parent owed. My voice carries beautifully and if I spotlighted one scofflaw parent, the others would probably snap right into line. I didn't think I was the kind of person who would do such a thing, but I could no longer remember what I was like before I sat at a pool five nights a week. I also really wanted to kick somebody in the ribs.

I also couldn't remember the last weeknight I had eaten dinner outside of my car—a car that, it should be noted, now smelled like chlorine and cheese burritos. Science has yet to provide a rearview-mirror dangle-thing to get rid of that particular miasma. But I believed this was a positive learning experience for Alice and no one could say she wasn't socializing.

On one especially chilly night, the kids were divided in half for a practice scrimmage. One of the older boys—the beefy kid who always hogged the ball—was hogging the ball. For five months I had watched him hog the ball, I'd watched the coach scream at him about hogging the ball and then I'd watched him hog the ball some more. Tonight he was modifying his game. Mostly, he hogged the ball, but on the few occasions he did pass it, he'd only pass it to his buddy. Alice and several girls were bobbing and waving directly in front of the goal, but he'd throw it to his friend who'd invariably muff the pass or miss the shot. I seethed. I'd spent months of increasingly cold and dark evenings standing out here trying to teach my daughter the value of teamwork, while this boy was teaching her the other side of the lesson—sometimes your teammates are flaming jerks. Then I'd go home, too tired and grumpy to have an icy drink encrusted with salt, and instead spend the evening scraping refried beans from the nooks and crannies of my steering wheel. I worked all day homeschooling my kid and I worked all evening muscling deadbeat fee payers. Alice's positive learning experience was making me very negative. And once again, the ball hogger passed the ball to his pal with the oven mitts for hands.

All of a sudden someone bellowed, "That is some seriously sexist shit!"

From the number of parents suddenly staring in my direction, I was led to understand the bellower was me. "Sorry," I whispered to no one in particular and attempted to shrink under a towel. Alice continued with water polo for another month, but that night marked the beginning of the end. The next time she asked to quit, I let her.

Which again circles back to the question, "What about socialization?" I guess the most accurate answer would have to be: Alice is doing quite well. I could use some work.

Cabin Fever

* * *

One morning in early January—January 3, to be exact—I drove past the local public school. I stopped at the light and gazed longingly at the flock of children swarming the front gate. Parents were standing around chatting, juggling cups of coffee, kissing their kids good-bye and heading off to work, home, errands. For the previous three weeks of Christmas break they had spent all their waking hours with their children, and now they were going back to the world of adults.

"The light is green," Alice announced from the backseat. "We should go skiing," she added. "Also, I'm hungry."

I navigated past the newly emancipated parents and restrained a sigh. This was not the week to ask me about the benefits of homeschooling. As I've mentioned before, when children homeschool they're always around. They aren't around as in: *The kids? They're around here somewhere.* No, they're around like it's the last day of summer vacation, and all their friends have gone back to school, and it's raining, and because you're the last hope for entertainment they reprise the entire repertoire of knock-knock jokes for the tenth time. They're *around.*

For the most part, I don't mind this around-ness. More often than not my daughter and I like each other, and even after months of not being apart more than a half day, we still find ways to enjoy each other's company. Also, her brain is young and elastic so she is able to remember that I did, in fact, buy cat food; I just left it in the trunk. That's the upside of having a constant little companion. The downside is that she is always around to remind me about the cat food and the trunk and anything else that springs into her mind. If our day-to-day life was a cable news channel, Alice would be the words scrolling constantly along the bottom of the screen. There's big Alice news, followed by small Alice news, followed by weather patterns Alice has noticed, followed by the news that a friend's parakeet escaped six months ago, followed by big Alice news, followed by a request for beans and rice. My brain is constantly toggling between the world in which I live and Alicelandia, where all subjects are equally worthy of reflection. All this toggling will eventually give me a brain hemorrhage. It's possible it already has. Here's an example of how this around-ness plays out in real life: Imagine Alice is in the kitchen, doing schoolwork and I'm sitting on the couch, reading *A Tale of Two Cities.*

(Please note: I didn't say I *was* reading *A Tale of Two Cities.* I said *imagine* I was reading *A Tale of Two Cities.* While you're at it, please imagine that I'm five foot eight, that my legs are too long and that I keep getting carded at nightclubs. Thank you.)

I open the book and begin reading. *It was the best of times, it was the worst of times, it was the—*

Alice drifts through the room, many feet from the schoolwork she's supposed to be doing. I look up from my book.

"Hi, sweetie."

"Hi."

"Did you finish your work? Do you need me to check it?"

"No."

A pause while we try to figure out which question she answered. I rephrase.

"The work is done?"

"Yes."

"Wonderful. Bring it in so I can see it."

"Oh. I mean no."

"Wonderful. Go do it, please."

Alice sighs and oozes from the room. I open the book again. *It was the best of times, it was the wor—* What is that noise?

"Alice, what are you doing?"

"My work."

"It sounds as if you're dragging a chair across the kitchen."

"I'm hungry. I'm getting some bread for a sandwich."

"Just finish your homework, please."

"But I'm starving!"

(Note: We ate breakfast a half hour ago.)

"If you're that hungry, get a carrot."

Silence. Offers of vegetables usually produce silence.

"I have a fun idea. Finish your homework."

"Fine!"

Sounds of a chair being dragged back to the table and a mumbled monologue about mothers who don't understand that bread-hungry isn't vegetable-hungry and how can someone possibly be expected to work while bread-hungry and nearly starving to death blah blah blah deedle blah. I reopen my book.

It was the best of times, it was the worst of times, it was the age of wisdom, it was the age of foolishness—

"Mom?"

Child at my foot. She looks remarkably alert for a person starving to death. She is holding a cat.

"Why are you here?"

"I don't understand something about my homework."

We troop into the kitchen, with cat, to examine homework.

"What don't you understand?"

"Why do I have to do it?"

Brief discussion on the benefits of learning to identify the parts of the cell. Longer discussion about the benefits of learning anything useful versus spending the afternoon hanging out with the cats, eating bread. Negotiations ensue. Seventeen minutes later, a child sits at the kitchen table writing out the words "Golgi bodies" in resentful strokes while gnawing on a jelly sandwich and ignoring a carrot. Her mother has returned to the couch and once again opens her book.

It was the best of times, it was the worst of times, it was the age of wisdom, it was the age of foolishness, it was the epoch of belief, it was the epoch of incredulity, it was the season of Light, it was the season of Darkness . . .

Wow, I'm actually doing it. I'm actually reading a book while Alice works quietly in the other room.

. . . *It was the spring of hope, it was the winter of despair, we had everything before us, we had nothing before us, we were all going direct to Heaven, we were all going direct the other way . . .*

Maybe I should be in there.

No. Wait. She needs to work independently to build work habits she'll cherish for the rest of her life. That's what that book said. Which book was that? Was it one of the books I liked? Anyway, it makes sense. She's working and I'm reading and we're both getting what we need. I could use a sandwich. But if I go in there I'll distract her and anyway, I don't actually need a sandwich, I just want one. Do we still have tapenade?

. . . *In the superlative degree of comparison only . . .*

What? Oh, I got distracted.

It was the best of times, it was the worst of—

Daughter is once again hovering near couch. She's carrying the other cat. "I'm done. Can I watch *Phineas and Ferb*? It starts in eight minutes."

"You're done?" I asked, cautiously.

"Yes."

"So I can check your finished work?"

"Wait. No."

We all troop back into the kitchen. There are twelve parts of the cell to label. When last I checked, she had identified two. Now there were three. It might be the best of times, it might be the worst of times, but it certainly wasn't the biology of times.

"I declare this science class over."

"Can I watch *Phineas and Ferb*?"

"Don't push your luck."

So now it's January 3 and we were in the car and she was talking about skiing, and how hungry she was, and what car she'd get when she turned sixteen, and how she thought her look for spring would be a flats-and-skinny-jeans look, and how hungry she was and maybe we could just stop by that Mexican restaurant we like and get some beans and rice? Unconsciously, I pressed my foot down a bit more firmly on the gas pedal so we could get home faster. Home meant Daniel taking over parenting. Home meant a bit of time off for me.

When I first started telling other parents we were going to homeschool, more than a few soberly informed me that the school system was a godsend, a life preserver, a benevolent force that prevented them from having to kill their children or sell them to an organ bank. After four months of this experiment, I could honestly say I hadn't once thought about killing my child or selling her parts for cash, but the excitement of the holidays was now behind us and we were facing a long, hard slog to June. Come to think of it, we were facing a long, hard slog to senior year. I might not have an afternoon to myself until well into the new decade. Sometimes I just wanted to cry.

". . . Which is why I won't go blond until after college," Alice completed her thought. In one reverie, I had missed thirteen years of my daughter's hairstyles. There was a pause. Clearly, it was my turn to say something. Considering I'd stopped listening over a mile ago, I went with a classic.

"Sounds like you've really thought this out."

Alice took a sip from her water bottle. "Now." She inhaled deeply, settling in for another mile or so of monologue. "What I plan to do with makeup will depend on whether I live in New York or Paris."

My phone beeped a text message. I handed it back to Alice, who stopped describing eyeliner long enough to read it. "Dad says he's running late. He won't be home until dinner." I bit my lower lip to keep from screaming. I had already called around; none of her friends were available that afternoon so it was just us. But she brightened at this turn of events. "Let's go to Nordstrom's and try on red lipsticks!" she bubbled.

And that was the day we learned a remarkable fact: Alice can be absolutely quiet for five blocks plus another half hour in her room if you give her the last three dollars in your wallet.

Then again, I seemed to be getting a few things right. Daniel had assumed responsibility over Alice's science curriculum, which improved the odds of her actually learning any science. This sounds too prefeminist for words—*Oh, those females and their inadequacy with math and science!* The truth is I really do like science. Of course, when I say "I like science" I mean I like to read about hideous medical afflictions, genetic disorders, nasty pandemics and other ghoulish topics related to the science of human imperfection. Several years ago, after I'd spent several nights in a row sermonizing during dinner about the late-stage symptoms of various plagues and the history of rats in Manhattan, Daniel had to declare a moratorium on my choosing what made for acceptable table talk. Sadly for me, the study of science requires more than images of supernumerary limbs and first-person accounts of virus-induced exsanguinations. Science is precise, exact, disciplined. I am none of these things. Daniel would teach our child the scientific method so she wouldn't adopt her mother's habit of waving a lazy arm toward an experiment and saying breezily, "N'yeah. Close enough."

With regards to math, I worked best as a cautionary tale. I can do a pretty decent job helping my child learn history. Same with English. But if forced to choose, I'd have to say our favorite class was hiking. I have often wished I were a natural dancer, an intuitive tennis player or skilled at any activity that required grace and feline speed. Instead, I'm a natural hiker. This means I have sturdy knees and an ability to plod along for long stretches of time and endure discomfort. When our school/house would feel a touch claustrophobic, I'd jiggle my keys and suggest a hike. Alice isn't a natural hiker. She is built more for skimming across the surface of a pond like a water bug than chugging up a series of switchbacks; but hiking wasn't school, and she's always up for things that aren't school. One convenient hike followed the canyon trail of a popular dog park so I could usually tempt her with promises of noneducation while in the company of affable unleashed dogs. We would hike and we would talk.

My initial plan was that we'd discuss whatever she was studying. This would make the intervals between pug sightings marginally educational. We would use the first part of each hike to revisit that day's course material, only in a more pastoral setting. It was the Socratic method with a Jamba Juice chaser. There's something oddly appropriate about discussing Washington's frozen winter at Valley Forge on a steep uphill grade. If one-quarter of all the

American soldiers died of exhaustion, disease and exposure, the least we could do while considering their plight was to pant a little.

Within a few weeks of commencing these lesson-hikes Alice figured out that while we were hiking, I was happy in a pack mule sort of way. After I'd quizzed her on the Trail of Tears or Shays' Rebellion and believed her sufficiently infused with the day's topic, I'd answer nearly any question she asked. I work on the assumption that if you're old enough to ask a question, you're old enough to get an honest answer, and the hikes were the most likely place to get me to blab about something I might regret later. Inside the house there are all sorts of disruptions to distract Alice from her pursuit of age-inappropriate Q&A. Sometimes I could be coaxed into a mother-daughter PG-13 dialogue in the car, but my answers typically slid into variations of: *"Alice, if I ever find out you text from the left-hand turn lanes like the bonehead in front of us, I will take away your license and drive you myself until you are fifty, and imagine what that would do to your social life and I mean it!"* But on a hike, everything was fair game.

So if you hike with your dog in Los Angeles, and at some point over the past year you thought, *How odd. It almost sounded as if that woman was rambling on to that innocent child about AIDS*, well, yes, that was me. In my defense, Alice had seen a huge billboard for HIV testing on the way to the park, which led to a discussion about AIDS. (When it comes to my daughter's education, I'm a staunch advocate of *the truth . . . and nothing but the truth*, but glide over the more awkward bits by promising myself I'll give her . . . *the whole truth* . . . in a few years, when we're both ready.)

On these hikes, we've talked about our criminal lack of closet space, divorce, the enviable hair of golden retrievers, religious differences and how to handle them with relatives over holiday meals, my inability to remember to bring a bottle of water for our hike and the larger issue of autonomy (which means Alice can remember to pack her own water bottle), the death penalty, the likelihood of our adding a French bulldog to our family, the electoral college and countless other things.

It should be noted here that it was Alice walking *me* through the workings of the electoral college. Again.

Does any of this matter? I hope I'm showing Alice the pleasure of wrestling with a large, complex topic without necessarily expecting to change a person's strongly held opinion or solve a thorny problem on the cheap. More likely, she's working me the same way students in any brick-and-mortar school will steer a naive teacher toward a pet topic to run out the clock or avoid a quiz. Either way, I'm sure she'd be just as happy standing at a Nordstrom counter, testing red lipsticks on her hand. On a rainy day, that's exactly what we'll do. But on days when the canyons are warmed by the sun and smelling vaguely of sage and strongly of dog, my daughter and I will pet a few mixed-breed puppies and hike away the hours talking of nothing and everything.

The Perils of Sensual Reading

* * *

It's a rare parent who doesn't want her children to inherit at least some of her belief system. Indeed, the pleasure—if not the obligation—of raising children is to instill in young, pliant minds those things that matter deeply to you. Owing to the sheer amount of time spent together, homeschooled children essentially marinate in their parents' core beliefs, no matter how baseless. They will accept as true the notion that if you ignore that grinding noise an appliance makes long enough, it heals itself. They will believe that salted caramels eaten quietly, alone, in a darkened garage don't contain calories. As adults, they might have to check hotel room closets for homicidal maniacs. Every day, your child registers a thousand invisible signals and catalogs a thousand hidden messages, none of which you've articulated in any explicit manner and very few of which are actually rational. Although I'd like to note for the record that my blender once made a grinding noise that I ignored, and it healed itself.

Now consider a student raised by parents who believe it is in the child's best interest to be exclusively taught by people who adhere to a specific and rigid ideology. A generation ago these children might have been exposed—in the classroom or on the playground—to attitudes and behaviors their parents found objectionable. They might have learned to defend their beliefs with conviction and vigor. Or they might have chosen to simply ignore other people's beliefs, or even to embrace them. In a shared school environment, young citizens learn how to work with, or around, the many contradictions that define modern society. That was the basic recipe of the melting pot, and many of us like to know it's still on the menu.

Today, however, a certain percentage of parents believe that modern society is a wicked concourse. For these people, every interaction outside the shelter of their religious community represents a potential ambush in the unending war between good and evil. In this war, children are corrupted by even the slightest exposure to sinful behavior, so the best option is to isolate them completely from the outside world. When I started writing about homeschooling on my blog I invited readers to share their experiences. One woman in her twenties from the Northwest wrote:

> My parents are super religious but in an alternate sort of way. If you call the organization they consider themselves to be a part of a cult, you would be in trouble because said organization sued

the powers that be some time ago and it was determined that they are a church, not a cult . . .

They pulled me out of school for middle school with the reasoning that they would be able to instill good religious beliefs in me, that I wouldn't be subjected to the liberal school system and its teaching of lies and that my most formative years, the puberty years, would not be spent experimenting with cigarettes and boys but at home.

At first I was relieved to not go to middle school. I would have been eaten alive. In retrospect though I don't know where I would have been worse off: being tortured in middle school or spending all day every day in the hell of my life at home.

My parents' religious teachings made me feel like it was my responsibility to care for them because they were family, that I wasn't a good person, I was guilty constantly, and so crushingly lonely I didn't know what to do with myself.

I just wanted friends and to be "normal." Escaping into books only helped a little. The rest of the time I had to contend with my mother and care for my sister and brother. I only have one memory of her actually trying to teach me something and she was wrong (the book was wrong according to her . . .) but it didn't matter and my lesson on ancient Egypt turned into some crazy story about demons and god and why women are punished with periods. I have a very good memory. I can remember crawling. I can remember almost all of elementary school. I can remember entire days just based on looking at a shirt in my closet. When I tell you this is the only memory, and quite probably the only incident of her actually "teaching," it isn't an exaggeration . . .

This woman's story haunted me for days. I know the Internet is a series of tubes filled with people who like to spin, embellish or lie outright but my intuition led me to believe this probably happened. In a certain way, a twisty helix sort of way, her parents' behavior would have been logical and consistent given the situation. If you believe the world is unsafe at any speed and that it means to cause your child real and permanent harm, you will seal up any aperture through which evil might find its way in. Of course, you'll also be sealing up any way your child might find a way out.

If the secret of homeschoolers is that most of them are just like your neighbors, the deeper secret is that some of them are like your neighbors, only more so. If your neighbors are a soccer family, the homeschool version can run kick drills for five hours a day if they so choose. If your neighbors push their children toward academic achievement, there's a homeschool version who drives three hundred miles to an academic decathlon swapping verses from *The Divine Comedy* in the car, in Latin, from memory. If your neighbors tend to keep to themselves . . . well, let me introduce you to the Gothardites.

When it comes to cultural isolation, you can't get much further off the grid than the Gothardites. Even if you haven't heard of them, you may have come across their reigning first family, a perpetually smiling Arkansas couple with (as of this writing) nineteen children and "very conservative values," who spread the gospel of a pure soul, a debt-free lifestyle and sexually segregated hairdos via basic cable. This is Christianity, all right, but it's a particularly American subset that takes the literal interpretation of the Bible to impressive heights.

In the early 1970s, an Illinois preacher named Bill Gothard founded the Institute of Basic Life Principles, a ministry of dauntingly broad authority over its parishioners. There's no aspect of domestic human activity Dr. Gothard doesn't cover in a book, a video program or a weekend retreat. Dr. Gothard* says the only path to salvation is to be "receptive to all the children the Lord gives," so birth control is strictly forbidden in any of its mechanical, pharmaceutical or chronological variants. This celebration of human fecundity is part of a larger Fundamentalist community known as the Quiverfull movement, a term based on Psalms 127/3:5:

Lo, children are an heritage of the LORD:
and the fruit of the womb is his reward.
As arrows are in the hand of a mighty man;
so are children of the youth.
Happy is the man that hath his quiver full of them:
they shall not be ashamed.

I am obliged to mention that Dr. Gothard has never been married and has no children.

As a follower of Gothard, it doesn't just stop with welcoming many, many arrows. In these families, not only does life begin at

* According to his official biography, Gothard received his PhD from Louisiana Baptist University in 2004. According to Wikipedia, LBU is "not accredited by an accreditation body recognized by the U.S. Department of Education or Council on Higher Education Accreditation." The university describes itself as "a primarily religious institution" that "has not sought either regional or national accreditation by a secular accrediting agency."

conception, so does Bible study. Gothard advocates that every mother read to her unborn child at least thirty minutes every day because the fetus can hear the word of the Lord in the womb and will absorb scripture through the umbilical cord, along with placental nutrients. If he's right, my pregnancy binge on *The Sopranos* was a potentially tragic choice. With any luck, my daughter will just be drawn to velour tracksuits and really good red sauce.

Once you've given birth to as many children as the Lord sees fit, and you've read to them in utero about Jonah's great fish in the Book of Jonah, the seven golden lamp stands in Revelations and the scores of foreskins in Kings, Exodus and Genesis, your next job is to raise them up. All Gothard families must observe the laws of patriarchy, which can be summed up as: *Do exactly what Dad says, always and without question.* Parenting is based upon a strict adherence to biblical directives and can include corporal punishment for children under the age of one. Girl children are raised to be submissive mothers and efficient homemakers. Boys are raised to support the presumably sizable families they will sire. If they choose, boys can attend a Gothard version of Boy Scouts called ALERT Cadets. The girls don't really have a version of Girl Scouts, probably because they are busy sewing modest clothes for their dozen or so siblings and learning to cook three meals a day for up to twenty people.

Gothard followers never date. At some point determined by God, a young man will approach a young lady's father and petition for courtship. If the girl's father agrees, the boy can visit his intended and begin wooing. Typically, an engagement will occur in a matter of weeks, a wedding a few months later. If the newlyweds have followed Gothard's strictures, their first kiss will transpire after the minister pronounces them man and wife, which might explain the accelerated timeline between hello and honeymoon.

Having wedded and osculated, the couple is now required to deliver into their quiver as many children as the Lord deems appropriate. They are also required to attend as many Gothard events as possible in order to maintain their blessings with God, meet other Gothardites and, one can only assume, introduce the next generation to its future mates. As the head of a Gothard household you are expected to work for yourself, ensuring that you answer to no one who isn't of like mind. You could, presumably, work for another Gothardite, but what if they were currently being plagued by temptation? Or what if on Wednesday they were godly but on Friday they were slightly less godly because the devil had their ear? After all, who would Satan desire more than these most observant of people? Best to remain an independent contractor.

Followers don't go to college because, according to the Gothardites, even the most upright Christian campus will include sinners whose profligate behavior is a potential source of spiritual infection. Worship at home. Teach at home. Only socialize with others who follow Dr. Gothard. And, despite attending many Gothard seminars (which are not cheap) and supporting all those children, incur no debt.

There are very few human undertakings that are not covered by a Gothard sermon, publication, video course or lecture, all of which profess the proper way to live. I have yet to find Gothard's advice on the proper way to die—I'm guessing at home, buried debt-free in the backyard—but that's my failing, not his. Any pastor who provides his flock with detailed shopping lists and suggestions on how to pick a dental plan wouldn't let them ad-lib death.

So you'll believe me when I tell you Dr. Gothard's writings are very, very clear about how his people should teach their children.

As luck would have it, he's created an educational program, the Advanced Training Institute, which only sounds like an organization run by the villain in a Bond movie. Gothard's ATI provides his adherents with twelve years of educational material, but it turns out these materials are only available to people who have signed up for the program. The website taunted me. I desperately wanted to see what they were teaching their kids. Perhaps I should apply, I thought, just to get a taste of the curriculum, like a Fundamentalist drive-through. I clicked open the application.

Name. Address. Email. Phone. Nothing troublesome here.

Your church, denomination, pastor. My first hurdle. We're regular churchgoers, but I'm pretty sure our version of God and their version of God weren't going to play well together. If anyone from ATI checked my church's website, he'd find troublesome words like "tolerance," "justice" and "acceptance." Better I say we church at home.

List all unmarried family members living in the home. Well, technically, that would include Daniel and me. Probably not what they're looking for.

Are any of your children resistant to enrolling? Since Alice has no idea I'm doing this, the answer is an easy no. Were I to explain that becoming a Gothard family could mean sharing one bathroom with up to twenty relatives, I'd expect some push back.

Is there anyone living in your home who is not a part of your immediate family? (If yes, please explain on a separate sheet of paper.) Don't want nonbelievers loitering in the shadows. Luckily, the only nonrelated boarders currently living with us are a dog and two cats. I've never asked, but my best guess is they're nonpracticing pagans. Better to leave them out for now.

Daniel walked by, glanced over my shoulder at what I was doing. Then he stopped and glanced again.

"No."

"It's an experiment," I whined. "I just want to see their workbooks."

Daniel stopped wondering about what motivated me a long time ago. Usually, his most negative responses to my little obsessions are: *No more than four pets in the house at any one time, thank you very much* and *We're still not getting chickens.* But every once in a while he gets his back up—and today, the back was up.

"Take me off that application."

"Fine."

I waved him off and calculated the odds of being accepted to the Advanced Training Institute if I were a plucky single mother raising her daughter alone. Question number seven asked marital status and, if separated or divorced, required a follow up essay to explain. Alice existed so Daniel had to exist. Or did he?

Father: Deceased.

I typed this in the box with what I hoped was a sorrowful font. If anyone were to ask, he died in a car accident last year. No, wait. Eight years ago. This is why I have only the one arrow and not a whole quiver's worth. It was so perfect, I nearly giggled. Sure, I'd miss Daniel, but his being gone in a tragic mishap solved a bunch of problems. Someday I'll stop to consider why I couldn't break up with him for the Radical Unschoolers but had no problem killing him off for the Gothardites.

Do you have a TV monitor in your home? I had read enough about

Gothard's followers to know they aren't allowed to watch television so I happily checked off "no," but the term "TV monitor" puzzled me. Is that like hall monitor? Or perhaps some sort of evangelical V-chip? Would that be a J-chip?

Does your family have daily times of Bible reading and prayer? Does each parent have a daily quiet time with the Lord? Do you have regular times of prayer together as a couple? Sure. Kind of. Define your terms. Fudge and waffle.

Has any family member been convicted of a crime other than a minor traffic violation? Finally, one I can answer honestly. I check "no" with a flourish.

Please check any of the following influences that are present in your home:

Alcohol Tobacco Occult/New Age materials

Video/computer games—hours per week:

Sensual reading/viewing material

Other

I'm saddened to realize that if the Gothardites are right, I'm going directly to hell and yet I have never taken full advantage of occult materials or sensual reading.

To the mother: On a separate sheet, please explain the basis of your salvation.

Oh, crud. An essay question. And not just an essay question, but an essay question I am completely unable to write, being as I'm more of the *I'd-sooner-walk-you-through-my-last-Pap-smear-than-discuss-my-personal-relationship-with-the-Unknowable* type of person. A small voice in my head said, "Quinn, someone has to write the worst salvation essay ever written and I'm pretty certain it will be you." My next thought was to crib some righteous testimony from a random Quiverfull family's website, but cheating at my faith seemed just the sort of thing to hasten the Rapture. Killing off Daniel for the sake of this ruse was no problem, but writing a fake essay about salvation gave me the heebie-jeebies. And yet I still wanted to see those workbooks, so tantalizingly close. So ripe with devotion. Was there no way to see Gothard's homeschooling material without . . . ?

Wait. I am *so* stupid.

Clouds parted. Angels sang. Shafts of light shone down from the heavens and illuminated the eBay icon on my computer. Someone somewhere had to be putting his eternal soul in jeopardy and cleaning out a garage at the same time. Two minutes later I had a list of strangers offering free shipping with my binder of self-guided salvation. Within hours, cartons of genuine Gothard/ATI material were winging their way toward my mailbox. For several days, I was extra-sweet to Daniel in silent contrition for almost killing him off on a wet freeway. For what it's worth, he would have died very suddenly. Never knew what hit him.

Children educated in the Gothard way study a series of workbooks called Wisdom Books. Each Wisdom Book is a self-published, large-format pamphlet about forty pages in length and covers one main topic as it intersects with science, history and literature. Sprinkled throughout each volume are vocabulary words, sidebar articles and illustrations that look as though they fell out of *My Weekly Reader*, circa 1958. Every Wisdom Book orbits a possibly meaningful central theme like "salt" or "law," but mostly they focus on religion, which is to say on the Gothardites' idiosyncratic version of Christian Fundamentalism.

In total, there are fifty-four Wisdom Books. I picked one at random. Wisdom Book #15 explores the subject of "light." There are scriptural passages referring to light, vocabulary words sharing the etymology of the word "light," some European history before the Reformation (you know, before The Light), a bit of science about the speed of light and a biology lesson on how sunlight creates food. This circling around a central theme is called "unit study" and isn't specific to Gothardite training. Many homeschool families educate using the unit study method. Of course, it's safe to assume most unit study texts on the subject of "light" don't include an in-depth discussion of sodomy.

To flesh out the concept of light, Wisdom Book #15 introduces an actual correspondence—at least what I assume to be an actual correspondence—between a concerned minister and the mayor of a large city in the upper Midwest. The concerned minister's initial missive complains that the mayor had given "official recognition and acceptance to the sodomites in the community." The mayor's response, reprinted in full, sparks an exchange with the concerned minister that continues through several pages, interspersed with vocabulary words, thought-provoking side essays and illustrations of biblical events in the lurid, melodramatic style familiar to anyone who studied art history at Bible college or attended a Christmas pageant staged by Brueghel the Elder. There are also "Questions for Evaluation," which present opportunities for parents and children to discuss the central themes in greater detail:

Does a person have no control over the sex to which he or she is attracted?

What does the original language say about "homosexuality"?

Are the scriptures unclear about sodomy and therefore open to interpretation?

Does God condemn "homosexuality"?

Notice how the word "homosexual" is always girded by quotation marks. It would be like describing a falling-down drunk as "tired and emotional" or a congressman under indictment as "resigning to spend more time with his family." You can practically hear the big eye roll inside every punctuation; oh, those crazy sodomites and their made-up words.

After the Questions for Evaluation, parents are encouraged to read "supplemental material on sodomy." Take heed, parents. I'm pretty certain this would land some readers right smack in the lap of sensual reading.

Immediately following the first Letters About the Sodomites section, the next vocabulary word is "mirror." I don't remember exactly when I learned how to sound out certain words, but I'm pretty certain I knew the definition of the word "mirror" before I knew the definition of the word "sex," let alone "sodomy." Having learned a new word, the Gothard student turns the page to find yet another volley in the epistolary exchange between the concerned minister and the mayor. Let us all stop right now to consider that the pastor's third letter includes a half page of footnotes. At this point we also should consider that whatever the mayor of Fargo, North Dakota, was being paid, it wasn't enough. Here again,

Wisdom Book #15 suggests we read the supplemental material on sodomy.

Then we get another vocabulary word: "Dependable."

On the next page, we see a picture: a Levite and a dead concubine draped across a primitive wheelbarrow. This is clearly a reference to . . . light? The perils of concubinage? Actually, neither. According to the caption, this is to further illustrate the horrors of sodomy. I began to wonder if, in the entire inventory of clip art, there was an image to illustrate the agony of a mayor who chose to answer his own mail. Wisdom Book #15 again recommends we read the supplemental material on sodomy, and also suggests that the student "write a letter to local government leaders regarding sodomy." It's not entirely clear, but I'm guessing the letter is to be *against* sodomy. The Wisdom Book further suggests that the student include the supplementary material to strengthen his case. I would suggest that the parents first check any laws which regulate sending such things through the mail.

And then a new vocabulary word: "Guide."

As with all the vocabulary words, the definition seems to be straight out of any dictionary and the etymology equally impartial. It's in the usage section where the fun really starts:

> **Guide:** as a verb—(to) guide, "Jesus promised that the Holy Spirit will guide us all to truth." As a noun—guide, "A defeated Christian who tries to be a guide to others is like a blind man leading blind men . . ."

After poring over stacks of homeschool catalogs and attending a Fundamentalist homeschool convention, I was pretty blasé about finding God in educational material. It's like "Where's Waldo?" where every person in the picture is Waldo. But Gothard's Wisdom Books stretch this to the point where the paper is Waldo, the ink is Waldo, the air is Waldo and you're Waldo.

Wisdom Book #15's section on science posed the question we've all asked ourselves at one point: *How does the laser illustrate the potential of unified Christians?* I'm not sure which answer they expect here. Mine would be: *Lasers, like Christians, are very constructive if used properly, but in the wrong hands have been known to burn holes in things.* There is also a supplemental booklet, called a Mastery Quiz, which includes a few dozen questions relating to each subject. I never got past question four: *What's the most effective way a Christian can demonstrate love toward a Sodomite?* My mind raced through a list of clerics and politicians far more qualified to answer this than I am.

Near the back of one Wisdom Book, under the heading Medical Resource, we learn "the ten ways to direct the eyes of others to your countenance" and how to "avoid eye traps." The latter lesson includes specific admonitions against "suggestive teasing, revealed skin, and fads." Rule 1 is "Wear a smile." Rule 2 is "Learn what season God made you," because God made us all unique and special but some of us can wear pastels and some of us shouldn't wear rust. Rule 5 is "Wear clothing that fits properly." It includes an illustration meant to show a young Gothardite male what well-tailored trousers should look like. This is compared to a rather detailed drawing of "too-tight" trousers, which, I suspect, is cross-referenced in the supplemental material on sensual reading. Rule 7 tells the reader to "Practice cleanliness and weight control." Rule 8 reminds us not to slouch. Rule 9 is to wear clothing appropriate to the event you're attending. Rule 10 is "Say the right things with your eyes," which I'm going to assume has nothing to do with sodomy. When it comes to the subject of appearance, Dr. Gothard is the aunt you avoid sitting next to at Thanksgiving.

As I explored this particular vein of highly regimented homeschooling, I found myself asking the same question over and over: What business is it of mine? We all make choices that we believe are right for our families. These families would probably look at my daughter and worry not only about Alice's education but also about her eternal soul. So let me say this: As long as they aren't hurting their children, how other people raise them is none of my business. I don't profess to be any kind of expert. Still, I can't help but be troubled by the power these authority figures have over their young charges.

If children are homeschooled within such rigorously enforced boundaries as those demanded by Gothard and his sort, every person these children come in contact with is singing the same exact tune. There is no second opinion. There is no pressure valve. The woman who wrote about being stuck at home with only her family understood on a visceral level that other ways to live existed beyond what her parents were allowing her to experience. She had interacted with the outside world for twelve years before she homeschooled for three, which gave her at least some sense of the alternatives. If the Gothard parents have their way, their children will only socialize with people who believe exactly what they believe and behave exactly as they behave, without so much as a visiting pastor—not to mention a science teacher—to interrupt the monologue.

We all shelter our children to some extent. We have to. The world isn't G-rated. When I keep Alice off certain fetid corners of the Internet or away from movies I know will disturb her imagination, I don't do it while rubbing my hands and cackling in delight over all the opportunities I'm forcing her to miss. I believe it's in *her* best interest to wait until she's older before she sees these things. So how is this different from parents who believe they have even more to fear than the loss of their child's innocence, that even a glancing exposure to sinful behavior could risk that child's path to eternal happiness? When it comes to protecting the hearts, minds and souls of our offspring, the line between *not enough* and *too much* is a minefield under the best of circumstances.

The problem is that children in ultra-authoritarian cultures grow up making no decisions on their own. There is never a point when you're considered old enough or mature enough to choose what you see, hear, think or feel. Truth comes to these children only through the Bible, through Dr. Gothard and through their parents. Education is an unrelenting chant to encourage conformity and obedience. Obey God. Obey your parents and elders. Obey Dr. Gothard. Follow the rules at all times or risk eternal damnation. If these children don't rebel, it may be for no other reason than that they lack the language to do it. This isn't just making a word verboten; this is making normal human impulses off-limits. Yet I also suspect this rigid style of childrearing actually undermines the intended goal of instilling kids with religious fervor. In order to feel passionately about something, it helps if you're allowed to question it from time to time.

This tribe would not have me as a member under any circumstances. I grew up in a gay neighborhood, moved to another gay neighborhood and then to yet another gay neighborhood across town because I feel most comfortable in proximity to irony and excellent cheese stores. I have a drink now and then. I've been known to wear pants. I selected our dental plan without consulting my minister. If they chose to, someone could correctly call my daughter a bastard. Until I attempted to fill out the ATI application, I would have sworn I was pretty boring. It turns out, however, that I'm quite sinful. So sinful, in fact, there is no way the Gothardites would allow me anywhere near one of their gatherings.

Which is why it suddenly became very, very important that I participate in one of their gatherings.

Driving this urge wasn't some perverse craving to be near a group of people who can't stand me. Lots of people can't stand me and I rarely insinuate myself into their get-togethers. No, in this case I was curious to see how many people actually showed up for a regional conference of the Advanced Training Institute. My comprehension of math is adorably childlike but I do understand that I have one child, and Quiverfull families are encouraged to have as many as they possibly can. It stands to reason that when Alice and her Quiverfull peers grow up, the Quiverfulls will field a larger team. But how much larger?

This particular group is incredibly secretive. The best estimate on the number of Gothardite families in the United States is in the mid–five figures, but that statistic is five years old. It could be more or less. And not all Quiverfull families are Gothardites—there are families who follow the biblical passage about procreation without following Gothard—which added a whole new layer to the convoluted Venn diagram dancing in my head.

Numbers aside, I had moved beyond mere curiosity about Gothard's followers into something approaching yearning. Once again, I longed to be among believers, even if I was nearly certain I wasn't going to believe what they believe. I wasn't going to rest until a tabernacle of Gothardites surrounded me. Best I gas up the car, assemble a prim little outfit, slap on a pious expression and go see for myself. But first, I needed to figure out how to get in.

Since I'm not a registered member of ATI, I couldn't simply buy a ticket online. My best option was to get to the Sacramento Convention Center and try to slide in somehow. Maybe I could insinuate myself between two families of forty or so people. If I did manage to infiltrate the conference, some legal-minded souls could describe what I was doing as trespassing. People get arrested for that, and I might never again be able to check "no" to the question about being arrested for a crime other than a minor traffic violation. On the plus side, there's probably a biblical passage that would dissuade the security guards from roughing me up, because that would involve touching and I'm not a wife to any of them. I am, apparently, a concubine, which means I'll eventually die in agony and be plopped in a wheelbarrow to illustrate the consequence of sin. Or light. Or something. Either way, I might as well have my strange little fun while I can.

I'd need something to wear. My Fundamentalist outfit wouldn't work because it covered my knees but revealed about four inches of calf which, for this group, would be as if I had wandered in from a 1987 Whitesnake video. A larger, looser dress would be required, but that wasn't going to be the most exciting part. No, for this excursion I'd also need long, chaste hair. I couldn't just buy a fake braid and tie it under a headscarf because it seems the Gothardites follow the biblical injunction against the wearing of braided hair. Luckily, there is a store in Hollywood filled with long, tumbling locks, curled and waved in every attractive fashion. One can also purchase translucent, six-inch heels and red vinyl hot pants at the same store, whose sign reads "Hottie-Z." I assumed no Gothardite would recognize a stripper wig or, if he did, wouldn't admit it. I located the perfect hairpiece in no time. At the counter, the customer ahead of me was getting a wig cleaned and restyled.

"Remember," she said to the owner, "it's Cinderella. So I need the curls right here." She pointed. "And here. Also, the ribbon has to be no farther back than *here*. They notice if it's not right."

I ventured, "Oh, you do kids' birthday parties?"

She blanked for a moment, and then answered in a slow, measured tone. "Sure. I mean, I *guess* I could." She then pulled out her phone and proudly showed me a few pictures of herself working as Cinderella. The blue bodice and puffed sleeves were exactly as I remembered from the movie. I suggested that if she started doing children's parties, she might want to wear underwear. Also, that pas de deux with the Fairy Godmother would need to go.

My outfit wouldn't be nearly as interesting: something loose on top and something long on the bottom. A quick trip to Goodwill got me a flower-patterned dress with puffed sleeves and a gathered skirt which in its previous life had either been a bridesmaid's outfit or a beach umbrella at the Junior League. It was five sizes larger than what I usually wear, rendering me female only in theory. Daniel declared it modest and awful. Alice kept worriedly asking me, "You aren't going to start wearing this all the time, right?" I was ready.

* * *

My instinct told me the best time to arrive undetected was after noon on the second day. The novelty of welcoming people would have worn off and, ideally, everyone would be sluggish from lunch and less aware of a bewigged beach umbrella in their midst. I arrived late in the morning, checked in to the hotel next to the convention center, got my hotel room, stabbed at the door with my key card until a housekeeper let me in, checked the closet for maniacs, put on my wig and my dress and bounded in a chaste way toward the Gothardites.

The main hallway was quiet as I strode virtuously past an empty table labeled "Registration." I slid into the main conference room, where about three hundred or so people were waiting for the next lecture to begin. Music played softly. One of Gothard's beliefs is that most music, even contemporary Christian music, encourages sin. Drums are specifically forbidden. You remember when you were little and stayed with your grandma and ate TV dinners and watched Lawrence Welk? It sounded like that, only without the lewd percussion.

There was a small bookstore set up in the back: familiar territory. On the top of one pile was a book called *All We Like Sheep*. Intrigued by yet another ovine-themed Christian book and hoping to find more helpful tips to avoid self-detonation, I flipped it open to find an enlightening little anecdote about how sheep manure is the best manure for a garden and the Lord is our shepherd and we are sheep. This, the book informed us, is what is meant in Psalms when it is written, "Surely goodness and mercy will follow me all the days of my life." It seems if you are the right kind of Christian, not only does your poop not stink, but it's excellent for compost. The Lawrence Welk music got louder, drawing us to our seats. Before the speaker began his presentation we sang a hymn, a cheerful, drum-free ditty about lamb's blood.

The lecture was about foiling procrastination or, more accurately, the speaker's definition of procrastination: putting off until later what God wants you to do today. The speaker had a book for sale in the back of the room, near the sheep-dung tome, which would help us with our own struggles with procrastination. In an effort to model good behavior, he told a story about how he'd promised God he'd never eat another cheese Danish because they were distracting him from his work and he never again consumed a cheese Danish and he's fine with that because while he has no cheese Danish, he has pleased God and has control of his appetites. He also has a book for going to bed and getting up using only your own self-control and not cheese Danish. It's based on scripture. It's available in the back. If we give him the names and contact information of three people we think might benefit from his teachings on not procrastinating, we'd get a free CD of time-management techniques.

I arrived expecting armed guards to keep me away from the received word of the Lord. Instead, I felt like I was attending a time-share condominium weekend. The speaker closed by saying, "The only question is: Will I obey God, yes or no?" He stared meaningfully down at the audience. "After all, delayed obedience is . . ." He stopped.

The audience answered as one voice, "Disobedience!"

There were a couple of arresting parts to that. First, they all answered in perfect call-and-response unison, leading me to wonder whether everyone on the planet knew this phrase but me, like maybe it was the first song on the White Album. Second, nearly every member of the audience was smiling.

People chanting in unison always make me a little edgy, especially when they're smiling. To distract myself, I fired up my modesty face and glanced around the room to take the measure of my fellow travelers. Demographically, I'd say the attendees were about 80 percent Caucasian, 19 percent Asian, 1 percent other (one African American family standing in for all the non-Caucasian or Asian races of the world). The speaker went on about other products of his we could buy to develop self control. My mind wandered. For the first time in my life, I really wanted a cheese Danish. For entertainment, I drifted to the back of the room to look through some of Gothard's pamphlets. Many of these books, ostensibly about education, were primarily about keeping a pleasant countenance, putting God first in all things and training yourself to see Satan, who is very skillful at disguising himself from the ignorant but totally obvious if you're paying attention. Reading through some of these paragraphs, I was reminded of Bugs Bunny confusing Elmer Fudd by wearing a dress and false eyelashes. Leafing through one pamphlet, I came upon a stern warning to avoid Satan's "tenicles." It would appear dictionaries, like drums, are also to be avoided.

I moved over to the table of books for teenagers, which held no truck with the newfangled notion that reading should be a source of pleasure:

Restraining Judicial Activism

Three Secular Reasons Why America Should Be Under God

And my personal favorite:

The Joyful Race to Rewards with a Cheering Crowd of Revilers

I can't wait to see the movie.

I began to notice a recurring numerical motif. Evidently, someone in Gothard's organization decided a numbered list soothes and enlightens followers. There were numeric references everywhere:

Five Steps to a Lifelong Intimacy with God

Seven Steps to Embrace the Word of God

Seven Steps to Maintain Moral Purity

Five Exciting Ways to Enjoy Your Family

Ten Ways a Husband Damages the Spirit of His Marriage

Five Steps to Getting Ready for Bikini Season

Okay, that last was just for me, but the other titles are verbatim. I was amused by how easily this group of people who live far outside the pull of worldly temptations, not to mention outside the pull of Seventh Avenue, could effortlessly begin writing slug lines for the cover of *Cosmo*.

Soon enough, it was five thirty and the scheduled dinner break.

I was tired and sweaty and my head itched. Modesty was uncomfortable. My hotel room suddenly seemed like a wonderful refuge. I slipped back upstairs and after a few hundred stabs at the door found a housekeeper to let me in. With a deep sigh of relief I peeled off my wig and looked in the mirror. In case you're wondering, hat hair is to wig hair as paper cut is to amputation. I switched on the TV and discovered nature's perfect antidote to a day spent with the Gothardites: a reality show about preadolescent beauty pageants. In one segment, a five-year-old with fake teeth and a spray-on tan was being prepped for the evening wear competition. She and I appeared to own the same wig. The camera loomed closer as this sequined princess lowered her mascara-swollen lashes and prayed, "Dear God, please make me win!" while her mother patted her exposed shoulder in solemn reverence. Once again in the presence of people for whom God was an active participant in their day-to-day lives, I found myself wondering what force was being unleashed here. Can absolute trust in a divine agent of consequence shift the wheels of destiny in your favor? Does this actually work? Will the Gothardites each have four score and seven children educated in a godly way and will Tawny win Little Miss Tulsa? Back on cable, the camera shifted to another pageant aspirant being reminded by her mother to "shake your little butt!" That might work, too.

After a while, I re-wigged and headed back downstairs to catch the evening program. As the dinner break ebbed, preadolescent boys cavorted boisterously in one corner of the lobby. In another corner, girls Alice's age played a more demure game of hide-and-seek. Across the middle of the lobby, teenage girls all dressed in black skirts and white blouses were herding a clump of preschoolers back to a playroom. The little ones walked in a neat line, their hands on the shoulders of the children in front of them like a conga line of hobbits. Watching them, it struck me that this may be the last time any one of them touches an unrelated person of the opposite sex until they are engaged.

The evening's lecture was to be given by Dr. Gothard himself. After a rousing drum-free hymn, the spiritual leader was welcomed to the stage by warm and enthusiastic applause. He was a small, avuncular turtle of a man in his late seventies with neatly coiffed hair the color of black shoe polish. His lecture was on *rhemas*—the overlooked secret of daily success. *Rhemas* heal all ailments. *Rhemas* make the weak strong. *Rhemas* erase spiritual doubts and cure leprosy. *Rhemas*, it would seem, can also turn a seventy-six-year-old man's hair jet black. And what are *rhemas*, exactly? Well, after twenty minutes of frantic note-taking and surreptitious iPhone searches mid-lecture, I came to conclude that *rhemas*, in this case, refer to the word of God. The term "Logos" also refers to the word of God. Both are good, but *rhemas* are better and you'll know a *rhema* when you see one. You might never have noticed a *rhema* before, but one day you'll be flipping through the Bible and *bam*! There's a *rhema*. Or *rhemas*.

And how will we know which part of the Bible is flinging a transformative *rhema* our way? We'll know with our spirit, which lives inside our soul, which takes up space inside our body. There was a drawing of this template projected on the screen behind him: a teeny heart inside of a well-demarcated soul surrounded by an amorphous and unappealing body. I noticed that nowhere in the schematic was there a brain. To the Gothardites, it would seem, a life of the mind is a weird and untrustworthy existence.

"Faith," said Gothard, tapping the dais in front of him with each word, "bypasses the intellect." In other words, if what someone tells you—or even what you experience—doesn't align absolutely with what Gothard has taught you to believe, then you need to pray more and think less. If Satan was going to invade any part of a Gothardite's body, it wouldn't be the pancreas; it would be the cerebral cortex. This educational model was designed to involve as little independent thought as possible because, hey, an eternity in hell is a long time to regret having looked at both sides of an issue.

At the end of the lecture, there was a wave of polite applause followed by a stampede toward the back of the room to purchase the reading material Gothard had recommended. Convinced there was no book titled *How to Make Your Hotel Key Card Work*, I left.

The next morning, I donned my beach-umbrella dress, popped on my wig and went off to find breakfast. I noticed with interest how wearing a highly modest ensemble makes people in line at a coffee bar smile nervously and start buttoning up their own clothing. The lecture for the morning was "Breaking the Mind-set That Hinders True Prosperity," which sounded especially relevant because I still don't have that beach house and wouldn't mind breaking the mind-set keeping me from that.

"The Israelites knew," the lecturer said, gazing around the room. "You do not make covenant with outsiders."

This wasn't a "Get to your beach house" lecture. This was a "Don't go to college and strangers are filled with damnation" lecture. University, we were told, is still public school. It is just as dangerous and subversive as elementary or high school because it's built on the Greek model. The ancient Greeks trained individual thinkers who were loyal to the state, but sacrificed morality and family loyalty in the process. We in this room should strive to be more like the Israelites and contain our lives within our own group.

"If you and your family syncretize to the outside world," he warned, "your children will marry outsiders. And they will be lost."

"The wolves were everywhere," he continued. "Even in places you would think would be nothing but sheep." At that moment I became acutely aware of my fake hair. The speaker went on to explain how Bible colleges are rife with moral corruption. They are to be avoided at all costs. A Christian homeschool co-op is no better. It could include families whose children don't dress modestly and might tease your children for doing so, and the next thing you know your daughters will be asking to wear pants. The only sure path is to stay within the Gothard group.

If you do attend college, you will leave with dangerous and irrelevant information, be laden with debt and forced to work for a corporation. And then, apparently, you will be indicted, I thought as the screen behind the lecturer filled with an image: a pair of arms in navy blue pinstripe, the wrists manacled. Superimposed text listed the horrors of the modern workplace. The first bullet point was *Forced to Accept Diversity*. "Stay within your people," the speaker urged. "Work for yourself." His own teenage children had no intention of attending college, he boasted, choosing instead to live at home and work part-time jobs where they could. They would bake pies to sell, give riding lessons and do plumbing, having learned it from YouTube. They would live at home until they married. If God didn't want them to marry, they'd live with their parents until they died. I hoped his children were happy. I was all but certain no one ever asked them if they wanted to live this way. I imagined towns full of houses, filled with people in their twenties, baking pies and waiting for their lives to start.

Suddenly I had a thought: Maybe anything as rigid as the Gothardite ideology can't hold up to actual use. Most of the brochures I saw featured a cover picture of Mr. Gothard speaking to a packed arena. Similar images were posted throughout the convention center but upon closer inspection it became clear they were all taken on the same day—about twenty years ago, judging by the clothes. The lecturer spoke almost wistfully of his first convention, where twenty thousand people filled an arena. We were, at most, two hundred families, with a surprisingly moderate average of three children each—fewer than one thousand followers, drawn from a region stretching from California to the Canadian border, and as far east as Arizona. Now, I'm pretty sure I couldn't persuade eight hundred people to pay to come see me speak, but I didn't start a religious sect that's currently in its third decade of encouraging unfettered propagation. If the first few years of operation saw the Gothardites fill an arena, they should now be filling a dozen. But they weren't. Perhaps people grow tired of being told they are not enough in God's eyes, or that they're failing, broken, damned by their lack of righteous fortitude. Perhaps people find it hard to interpret "blessed are the poor" as God's instruction to have so many children that you can't budget more than sixty-five cents a meal to feed each one of them. Perhaps people suspect it's not spelled "tenicles."

The speaker wrapped up. I walked outside. A young woman in a slightly-shorter-than-everyone-else's skirt was talking intently to an older couple. "I was listening to him speak," she said, "and I realized he was totally right. A college education isn't worth it. I am completely embarrassed to be going to Berkeley."

I froze in my tracks. First, of all the universities I might expect to hear name-checked at a Gothardite convention, the institution that gave us the Free Speech Movement and political nudity was not one of them—unless under a seminar listing called "Sinful Places We Don't Even Think About." Second, this young woman wasn't reverse-bragging about attending one of the most sought-after universities in the United States the way some people bemoan their hummingbird-rate metabolism. No, she actually meant it. She was mortified to realize she would be "wasting my time when I should be learning something I can do from home." The older couple nodded in earnest unison. "Who needs another architect?" the girl added despairingly.

Her question robbed me of the comfort I had taken in noting the Gothardites' unimpressive numbers. I wandered past an open meeting room where about two dozen teenage girls were being taught a game by a handful of girls a few years older. The younger girls would find a partner and link arms. One girl was then chosen to run among the group and link her arm with the outside arm of one of the paired girls. This would make the new girl and the linked girl partners, sending the third girl, now a free radical, off into the crowd to break up another pair. The teams shrieked and dashed around in their long skirts, trying not to get caught. I doubted it was a coincidence that the point of the game was to create paired partners, and the most dangerous element was an unmatched female. And I found myself feeling very sorry for these girls.

From what I had overheard in conversations, most of these children had been born into this life, but their parents hadn't. At some point, the adults had chosen to sequester themselves. The parents might not have liked the world outside but they had lived in it for a while. They knew what was out there. These children didn't even know what they didn't know. This was a community where one of the few topics of debate was whether a mother could teach her son once he reached adolescence or had to stop teaching him because no woman could tell a man what to do. Each generation might know a little less than the generation before. One of these laughing, running girls might have a natural inclination toward science; with the right education and some hard work, she might discover a new antiretroviral drug, saving untold lives. If she remained with the Gothardites, she wouldn't. One of the preschoolers I'd seen earlier might have a talent for dance, or playing the drums, or drawing anime. If his family stayed with this group, he would never know about something that might have filled him with passion or given him purpose beyond breeding and worshipping God. These children would never have the chance to explore what they could be, only to follow the narrow path to what they must be.

My dress was hanging heavily on my shoulders and my wig felt tight. My countenance certainly wasn't smiling. In all ways I could measure, I was done with this adventure. I took one last look at the young women and left the building, eager to get back to the real world.

Oh, What a Night

* * *

One of the advantages of homeschooling is that you can see your family doctor or dentist during the less popular hours. Let the traditionally educated battle over the après-school appointments with the pediatrician; we'll slide right into the office for a checkup at 11:10 and be out by 11:30. It's glorious. Except for when it's not. Like the time I rolled through a stop sign and got a ticket.

As I pulled over, my mind raced. It was midday. I had a school-age child in the backseat, obviously not being educated. Could I prove we homeschooled? Was there a half-finished educational workbook somewhere in this car? Would I finally meet my very first truant officer? Wait, we were fine. If he asked, I'd say we were on the way to the doctor's office, which was true. He would assume she was sick. Alice was reading, which with any luck had made her slightly motion sick; a nauseated appearance would strengthen my case.

He leaned in the car, asked for the usual bits of paperwork. He saw Alice in the back, leaned in a little farther and asked her in an offhand cop sort of way, "Why aren't you in school today?"

"I homeschool!" she chirped brightly and healthily and promptly went back to reading.

Would it kill me to come to a complete stop?

The officer stopped writing, looked at me enigmatically through his sunglasses and asked, "But what about socializing? What about going to prom?"

Over the seven months that we'd been homeschooling, the questions about socialization had not abated. Wherever we went, people continued to broach the topic, their tone of deep concern sometimes offset by a faint whiff of snideness. And at least half the time, by question three, they'd be asking about prom, which always seemed unnecessarily foresightful considering how Alice was closer to nap age than prom age. The questions went something like this . . . Actually, they went *exactly* like this:

"Do homeschoolers have a prom?"

"Where do they hold their prom? In the den?"

"And who do they take to the prom? Their *mother*? Bwahahahaha!"

The cop chuckled to himself, obviously pondering the absurdity of a homeschool prom. Because homeschoolers are now sort of my people, I felt a little sad and protective. My mouth reflexively began to say something about how slightly eccentric but basically familiar homeschool proms are, but before I could say anything, I was cut short by the brutal realization I had no idea what I was talking about. I didn't know what a homeschool prom looks like. I wasn't even certain they exist. I had a creeping fear that if they do exist, I'd unearth websites featuring pictures of teenage boys escorting women in their forties with captions like *Pinning the corsage . . . Oops!* and *No doubt about it, my mom was the prettiest girl in the room!* There might be a video of the evening's last dance: a rousing hokey-pokey at nine fifteen, before everyone returns home to play Jenga. It might not be as bad as the snickering cop suggested. Then again, it might be worse.

Since Alice was still many years away from a prom invitation, I went online to see what I could find out. I searched the phrase "homeschool prom" and scrolled down the options. California had surprisingly few listings. Southern California had only one, and it was limited to students from a specific program. Fortunately, the Midwest and Southeast were hotbeds of prom-itude, listing at least six proms open to anyone who homeschooled. Most promised wholesome fun and chaperones. That's it! I would offer my services as a homeschool-prom chaperone. Now, the hard part: How could I offer up these services without coming across as the sort of person who wants to spend an evening in a distant city staring at unfamiliar teenagers?

I sent the following email to six prom coordinators:

Dear Prom Coordinator,

My name is Quinn Cummings [true]. *I homeschool my daughter* [true] *and I am surprised to discover there are no organized proms*

> *for homeschoolers in Southern California* [true, this did surprise me]. *Several homeschool parents and I are thinking of creating a prom like yours* [true-ish. I was thinking about proms in the abstract and I assume other homeschool parents were also doing the same, or at least enough to satisfy the definition of "several"], *and I'd love to help chaperone yours and see how it all comes together* [true]. *As luck would have it, I will be traveling through* [Illinois/Missouri/Alabama/Indiana/Florida] *the week of your prom* [true. If they invite me to chaperone, I'll be traveling through their state]. *Blah blah, polite windup, yours truly . . .*

I guess the peculiar leaked through a bit more than I would have liked because four of the prom coordinators didn't bother to respond at all, and one wrote back saying something like, "Couldn't be more generous of you to offer, but you're a complete stranger and possibly a predator and I can feel you inappropriately touching our children from here." Writing back and explaining that I was the harmless kind of eccentric was certainly an option, but I didn't think it would lead to an invitation to chaperone. So I had pretty much given up on the whole business when I received an email from the last prom on my hit list, from the very aorta of the heartland. They could use help. They'd love help. Could I call them the next day? This was perfect. I had twenty-four hours to practice not sounding too creepy on the phone.

Let me introduce my prom coordinators. "Elizabeth" and "Jane" are sisters. They were seventeen and fifteen years old, respectively, and they were adorable. They referred to me as "Mrs. Cummings." During our first phone conversation, Elizabeth said tentatively, "But, Mrs. Cummings, you do know our prom is . . .

traditional, right? It might not be what you're used to out there in Los Angeles."

Frankly, I was relieved to hear it. I had never chaperoned anything before. A *traditional* prom might present its own challenges, but I suspected I'd be less likely to find an attendee giving birth in the coatroom. Elizabeth continued, "And we're asking both the guests and the chaperones to dress conservatively." She sounded hesitant, but I took no offense. Los Angeles is known for having many denizens who go to semiformal events and forget to wear underwear.

Now on the list, I received a prom-centered email from the girls every week. If you lived locally, there were dance lessons available. You could learn to do the reel, the Cotton-Eyed Joe and several dances which sounded like euphemisms for activity a chaperone might find unsettling: the Cupid Shuffle, Slappin' Leather and the Cha-Cha Slide. These were all group dances that could be enjoyed without getting too close to another reveler. There would be chaperones placed everywhere there were teenagers: the hallway, the ballroom and the bathrooms. The instructions for my dress arrived. Everyone, prom guests and chaperones alike, were to abide by the same rules: no plunging necklines, no skirt (or slit) cut higher than mid-thigh and nothing see-through. We chaperones were to monitor the dress code as each guest arrived and periodically thereafter as the evening progressed.

As luck would have it, I owned a black dress that I thought was modest, respectable and above reproach. I'd bought it several years ago for a very chic dinner party and worn it exactly once. In the store it looked modern and sleek. As soon as it left the store, it mutated into a shroud with cap sleeves. Wearing this dress, I became an undifferentiated mass from collar to hemline. I was a black satin tube of toothpaste. It was perfect.

Three weeks out, my chaperone instructions arrived. Two pages, single-spaced. They expected about one hundred and fifty guests and ten chaperones. That seemed a little chaperone-heavy to me, but I was in a car accident on the way to my prom and spent the night in an emergency room instead of a ballroom, so my knowledge of such things is limited to hearsay. Also, this was a Christian homeschool prom in the middle of Indiana, which might explain the breadth and depth of supervision called for. The following passage was noteworthy: *Girls can dance with girls for the group dances. There is no reason for boys to dance with boys—there are lots of unescorted girls!*

I sensed a slightly elevated tone in that last bit, and perhaps a nervous laugh. If there is any reason a young man might be thinking about dancing with a friend, it must be because he hasn't noticed all those lovely unescorted girls he could ask! Right?

As the date approached, I still couldn't answer the question: Was this going to be a typical homeschooler prom? Was this going to be the same as a typical non-homeschooler prom? I brought the chaperone's rules of engagement to a friend who had attended an evangelical Christian high school. She scanned the list and handed it back. "Imagine this evening without dancing. That was *my* prom," she said, sighing. "And forget earrings. Earrings were strictly forbidden." Nowhere on my list was there anything about jewelry, but I packed smaller, more demure earrings just to be safe. A too-large earring might cause man-on-man dancing to break out.

To save money, I had cunningly booked myself on a cheap connecting flight, not considering that this got me into Indianapolis at four thirty in the afternoon. I was due in the ballroom at five thirty. The hotel was a half hour away, so it made sense to change at the airport and head straight for the prom from there. I dragged my bag into the bathroom, tugged on the dress, hoiked up the black nylons, stepped into my heels. I'm going to assume not many people walk around the Indianapolis airport in a black satin dress and heels, fewer still when it's still daylight outside. From the expressions of the women in the ladies' room who watched me put on my makeup, I can only assume I'd just become the star of their soon-to-be favorite travel anecdote: "That time I saw a whore at the airport."

I grabbed the first cab, raced to the hotel and checked in. I was handed a key card, which I stabbed at my door a few dozen times until a passing housekeeper let me in. I flung my bags on the bed, checked the closet for homicidal maniacs, turned around and raced to the location. The prom was to take place in a ballroom on the top floor of a local building. The prom was to take place in a ballroom on the roof of a commercial building from the 1920s. The ballroom was designed by someone trying to create the effect of an Italian piazza without benefit of ever having visited Italy or, for that matter, anyplace outside of central Indiana, and yet it was adorable in a plastic grape sort of way. Elizabeth and Jane were there along with the other chaperones, most of whom were related in some way. I became excruciatingly aware that I was the only woman wearing a dress that revealed anything above the ankle. The people at the airport had it right.

Elizabeth and Jane, the evening's hostesses, were charming, pink-cheeked and ebullient in full-skirted dresses the colors of tropical flowers. Their family was lovely and politely welcoming.

Their mother was pregnant with number nine. Another chaperone was pregnant with number eight. Until this moment, I would have imagined that by the time you were chaperoning your daughter's prom you had thrown away your nursing bras.

We were given a brushup on what did and didn't constitute acceptable physical contact between guests and what constituted a modest prom dress. Breasts were to be supported and covered, no cleavage below the natural bra line, nothing sheer. "Girls," another chaperone said firmly, "don't need to be showing things meant for their husbands." I was sent to the balcony to observe the dance floor from above—aerial reconnaissance among the plaster cherubs—and also to prevent anyone from having anything resembling fun in the balcony. This turned out to be an easy assignment because not one couple tried to sneak upstairs. Perhaps they had been warned away by rumors of a black-clad whore exposing her calves up there.

While waiting to kill fun, I looked around, trying to figure out if this was just like any other brick-and-mortar Christian high school prom. Gowns were being admired. Pictures were being snapped. Kids were texting, giggling and hanging on to one another. The girls, anyway. The boys without dates stood around, talked softly and did things like retie their shoes and stare discreetly in the girls' direction. Boys with dates stood around and watched their dates text, giggle and hang on to one another. It seemed pretty familiar. About half of the parents stayed for a while, smiling and admiring their children, who, to my amazement, didn't seem to melt into a puddle of horror under such scrutiny. This behavior alone differentiated these kids from most teenage gatherings I've experienced. But something else was different. Something was missing. The room had a strange vibe. I stood at my post and took in the scene below.

Finally, I figured it out. It was the boys. They didn't swagger. I have several friends with teenage sons. If more than three of them are together in one place and there is anything resembling estrogen in the air, they all begin to swagger. They can't help it. And along with the swaggering comes the shoulder punching and the doofus shouting and it all becomes this lovely, loud dance to draw the attention of a person who is studiously ignoring them while twisting her hair and biting her lip in a winningly disinterested fashion. It's sweet and obnoxious and utterly predictable. Except there were easily fifty young men down there, some alone, some with a date and some in groups, and not one was behaving like a stag in rut. Was this because they were homeschooled? Was it because they were socially conservative Christians? Was it because no one swaggers in Indianapolis? Wait, that's absurd. They must swagger in Indianapolis. What is the Indy 500 but one endless, gasoline-scented swagger? And yet the evidence in front of me said otherwise.

In some ways, the entire evening was about sex. Sure, it was about no-sex, but if you're constantly guarding for any potential outbreak of sex, it becomes an evening about sex, only in reverse. It was like a Zen koan: What is a mating ritual without mating?

I passed by one chaperone explaining to another that her son liked to salsa dance at home, "but not the sensual kind." Must be that shoulders-up salsa dancing I've been hearing about. The most troublesome couple persisted in sitting together holding hands. At one point, the boy stretched out his arm and put it over his date's bare shoulders. He was sitting on a couch in the area I was assigned to monitor. Witnessing this, the other chaperone assigned to this area and I were stunned into silence. They were touching. He was touching bare skin. But it was the back of her shoulders and his arm was covered in a jacket. But they were in the main room, in plain sight. This had to be wrong. I have been in clubs in Los Angeles where people appeared to be making new little club-goers in the next banquette, but after three hours here, I was genuinely unhinged by something that wasn't even first base. I turned to the other chaperone and whispered, "That's sinful, right?"

The other chaperone hissed, "They've been testing us all night. That just *ticks me off.*"

She strode across the ballroom and sat down next to them. At that moment, another girl approached me to ask a question, and by the time I looked back up, the chaperone was returning toward me, smiling pleasantly. The touching couple was now in separate chairs, examining the floor. "Bless you," I whispered to her. I didn't want to fail at the only task I'd been assigned all evening. Nor, would it appear, do I ever want to tick off a good Christian woman.

The choreographed dances were designed with an eye toward making teenagers very tired without touching anything more suggestive than a wrist bone. These were dances Jane Austen would have recognized—a fair amount of energetic skipping and linking of arms, faces flushed by synchronized footwork and perhaps just a breath of belladonna. The point to these dances was to create such a level of gasping, sweating and fatigue that, hopefully, the participants couldn't think of anything else that might cause gasping, sweating and fatigue. During the free dancing, we chaperones wandered throughout the group, ever ready to glare sin into submission when the choreographed dances hadn't tired them out enough. I don't know where the teens' minds were wandering, but I can tell you their hands stayed on absolutely neutral body parts, and those bodies had about eighteen inches of personal space between them at all times. Not so much as a free-floating rib was molested.

In the final hour, I was assigned to chaperone the powder room. In the vestibule there was a chair with a sewing kit on the armrest. After seven hours in three-inch heels, I sank gratefully into the chair and glanced nervously at the sewing kit, praying I wouldn't actually have to mend something as I have no sewing skills besides sewing a button back on. If a dress tore, or was deemed too revealing, my suggestions were going to be limited to: "Let's put four hundred seventy-three safety pins in it," "Do you need a button sewn on?" or "It's probably best you just go home." Along with the sewing kit, Elizabeth and Jane had thoughtfully put a basket of hair products next to the mirror, which meant that nearly every girl came in and freshened up her hair when she didn't feel like doing the Virginia reel. By the end of the evening, the collective height of the hairdos increased by about three yards and the bathroom resembled a foggy night in Victorian London, only peach-scented. By the time I arrived several girls had just settled in, chatting with each other and trying out new hairstyles. I rubbed my feet idly and listened to them talk.

You know what nice, conservative Christian girls talk about when they do each other's hair at the prom? They don't talk about boyfriends because they don't have boyfriends. They don't talk about after-parties because they don't have after-parties. They don't gossip about the other girls at the party because nice Christian girls don't do that, or if they do, it's done with majestic subtlety. No, what these girls talked about while they did each other's hair was . . . hair. Twenty-five minutes later, having inhaled enough aerosol lacquer to glaze a haystack and having heard every single perspective on the subject of rinsing one's hair in cold water to make it shiny, I broke into their conversation.

"Excuse me?"

Four doe-eyed girls in covered cleavage turned toward me as one.

"Ma'am?"

"Have any of you gone to another prom? I mean, like a regular high school prom?"

Two girls shook their heads and said, "No, ma'am," firmly. One said, "Yes, ma'am. I go to a Christian school and we had a dance."

The last girl leapt in and said, "I go to a public school. My prom was last week."

"So, was it like this?"

They looked around the bathroom, at each other and the droplets of hairspray suspended in the air. One said, slowly, "You mean was it like this bathroom?"

I clarified. "Was the school prom like this . . . outside?"

The Christian school girl thought and then shook her head. "No, ma'am. This was way more fun."

I turned to the public school girl, who said, "Well, no. I mean, this is really nice and everything, but, like, we didn't learn dances or pray before dinner at our prom. This is different."

The door opened and a new girl slipped in, bringing some of the music into the bathroom with her. The public school girl said softly, "But it's nice here. I feel like . . . a lady."

* * *

The prom ended at midnight. At 12:10, the hotel would start charging a late fee. The chaperones hustled the guests out in a modest but firm way toward their parents, who had come to collect them. The waitstaff started breaking down tables before the last gown shuffled out the door. The hosts wrote the fiddler a check. Prom was over. I thanked Elizabeth, Jane and everyone involved for letting me participate. A prom guest walked past me in the elevator lobby. Her hair, which had been up in a high bun all evening, was now tumbling down her back, returning the elegant young ingénue back into the fifteen-year-old girl she was. A word chimed into my brain: transformation.

Adolescence is a cascade of changes and transformation. There is no part of a teenage body that doesn't change drastically over these six or seven years. Many aspects of this metamorphosis are pleasant and entertaining, but to anyone going through it, the absolute lack of control over the process can be unsettling. For this one night, teenagers get to have some say over the changes that have been rocketing through their lives. For one night, they are stars in their own movie while we, their parents, watch from the sidelines, cheering on this newfound pride in themselves and their wobbly first steps in the ultramarathon of adulthood.

I had just spent the evening in the middle of Middle America with a hundred and fifty homeschooled kids at a ritualized social event that each is unlikely to forget. Did it meet their expectations? Hard to say. Was it a prom?

It most certainly was.

Mapquest

* * *

As our year of homeschooling stumbled toward the finish line, I began to wonder: Did this work? Had I (and Miss Stephanie the math tutor, and Madame Rose the French tutor and Daniel the science parent) proved ourselves able to educate Alice to the best of her potential? To the best of *our* potential? Did we provide my daughter with a better learning experience—academically and socially—than the other schooling options available to us last September? Or should I have stayed in the laundry room, sucking my own exhaust?

I began my first teacher evaluation with items I could easily measure. Alice had completed slightly more than one academic year's worth of her math curriculum in just under nine months. She displayed only slightly less loathing for the subject than when we started, but she could calculate tips in restaurants, double any recipe ingredient in her head and determine the area of a triangle (which I, sadly, could not). I recalled a recent morning when she was working on a problem about two trains leaving a station at differing rates of speed, the solution of which required long division with remainders. She whipped through that once-dreaded process in a matter of seconds.

"I don't know why I was so stubborn about these," she said, more to herself than to me. "They're kind of fun in a weird way."

I stood as still as a rabbit with a hawk circling overhead, basking in a rare moment of self-congratulation. My silent whoop of elation must have registered in Alice's deepest brain cells, because she quickly glanced up and added in a flat, defiant voice, "But I still hate this stuff."

Message received. Beaming on the inside, though.

She continued to consume books like an industrial shredder, reading at least one a day. Thanks to a great neighborhood library and a generous bookstore friend who provided Alice with prepublication copies of children's books, this did not send us to debtor's prison. Volumes of every shape and size were piled like ziggurats around the house, adding a festive touch to our already chaotic décor. In exchange for the advanced copies, Alice was asked to prepare a short review of each book, ostensibly as consumer feedback for the publishers but actually as encouragement for her to continue writing. Looking back at Alice's book reviews over those months, I could track how her writing had improved in both style and substance, despite a recurring complaint that every book she read would have been improved by a strong female protagonist with the ability to shape-shift into a cat.

With her father's help, Alice kept a science notebook in which she'd demonstrated that she could form hypotheses, create experiments and analyze results. Thanks to her mother, Alice had an impressive knowledge of the flu pandemic of 1918, and she knew the difference between porphyria (the disease which might have caused the madness in George III) and progeria (the genetic mutation which causes people to age rapidly and die in their teens). Let other mothers and daughters bond over scrapbooking or a vegetable garden; Alice and I shared a fascination with the strain of hemophilia in Queen Victoria's descendants. She could also differentiate between acid and alkaline, work a microscope and discuss Ebola-induced exsanguination over a breakfast of soft-boiled eggs. Were I running the world, this would be the definition of a well-rounded individual.

As far as French went, she seemed to know several more ways to tell me she was hungry. Also, she continued to sound nothing like me speaking French, and that was good.

After the Portugal Problem, I'd become obsessed with ensuring that Alice be able to identify all the states in the United States and most of the more popular, if not populous, countries in the world. I would lie awake at night, unable to shake the image of the American high school student who, when asked to find China on a map, pointed to Vatican City. When I did fall asleep, visions of Chairman Mao wandering lost in St. Peter's Basilica began to haunt my dreams. There was no way my daughter would become a geographical punch line. I was going to fix that right away.

Yet besides buying the atlas-themed placemats, I'd done nothing. Instead, I took a page from the unschoolers and hoped the volume of historical reading that Alice had been doing, both fiction and nonfiction, would somehow leech all those map inserts and fancy frontispiece illustrations into her head. The risk of this plan was that she might confuse Atlanta with Atlantis, or locate Luxembourg next to Rivendell. Around the end of April, I gave Alice several blank maps and asked her to fill them in. She squinted at me and said, "Is this a test?"

"Yes," I answered dryly. "Of me."

"Then you should take it, too," she said.

Instantly, my old nemesis, the Little Voice in My Head, showed up. "What a marvelous idea!" it announced. "You should ask Daniel to take it as well, so that everyone can bask in your shame!"

On the map of Europe, I named ten out of fifteen countries correctly. Four of those were Italy, Russia, France and England—the cartographic version of getting two hundred points on the SAT because you filled in the right bubbles beneath your name. Ten out of fifteen isn't so great, especially when you consider there are forty-nine countries in Europe. And I'd scrawled "England" over several proud countries that aren't, in fact, England. Alice did better, but not by much. Let us note the placemats did both of us some good; we both knew where Portugal was.

Daniel got forty-six out of forty-nine, including Belarus. Alice and I slid down in our seats. Hoping to restore a gnat's worth of dignity, I next handed out blank maps of the United States. We all set to labeling.

Daniel knows his states.

Alice knows her states.

I forgot Wyoming and Nebraska as if they never existed. I might as well have scrawled "Here Be Dragons" across several million acres south of the Canadian border. I put Minnesota in one of the Great Lakes, which is especially distressing when I stop to consider that my mother grew up in Minnesota and her family has lived there for nearly two centuries. Out of ignorance, or some Freudian impulse, I had drowned my ancestors.

We finished writing and everyone stared in wonder at my map. Even across the kitchen table my map looked sparse and tentative, like a badly shaved leg. Finally, Daniel said, "You're just tired." Alice offered, "I can quiz you, if you like."

I looked down and realized I had also forgotten Utah and Alabama. The Little Voice had another idea, and for once I let her speak for both of us.

"Let's study this in the fall," I said out loud.

We all looked at each other in silence. Daniel and I had discussed next year's schooling, but only after Alice went to bed at night. Alice and I sometimes alluded to next year's schooling on our walks. I assumed Daniel and Alice might have discussed next year's schooling at some point but this was the first time we were discussing it together as a family. We continued to look at each other.

"So," Daniel said, finally. "We're staying with this?" It was a question, not a statement.

"I don't know," I said. Then we all fell silent again.

Here was the problem: Alice had clearly flourished as a homeschooler, but I still had my doubts. I was no more certain of my tribal status than when we started this adventure. I admired the unschoolers' confidence and spirit but if the family map quiz taught me anything, it was that the location of Montenegro probably wouldn't enter anyone's head by osmosis. Some subjects require the mallet of instruction. I could appreciate the Fundamentalists' conviction that knowledge is good but faith is better, but I didn't want Alice learning that way. I could even empathize, sort of, with what sent the Gothardites down that particular rabbit hole. When you're anxious about life's eternal consequences, the idea of a narrow path leading to a place of guaranteed comfort and safety seems very appealing—assuming you don't miss the lovely brain you had to jettison to make the trip.

I had cobbled together a version of homeschooling for Alice, trying to avoid infecting her with my own academic weaknesses in the process. So far, this improvised methodology seemed to be working reasonably well. What worried me now were the far horizon and the bigger questions. What if we were *all* wrong? What if all of us homeschooling parents—unschoolers, Fundamentalists and improvisers alike—were producing a generation of children unable to participate in a world where growing economic turbulence makes the potential for failure far greater than any hope for success? When too many qualified people compete for a single job, employers assign great weight to subtle indicators of status, including "Where did you go to school?" Maybe the one thing the various homeschooling tribes shared was that, contrary to our best intentions, we were screwing our children out of the most fundamental right of young adulthood: the right to opportunity. Maybe I was destroying my kid's future.

Yet how could I ignore how happy Alice seemed to be lately? How could I write off her newfound enthusiasm for learning, her emerging poise and the way she tackled life's large, ambiguous questions while we hiked the canyons? How I could I argue with President Garfield?

Back in November, I had the sudden realization that a TV

game show in which the contestants spend twenty-two minutes spewing random facts under pressure could be construed as educational, so I introduced Alice to *Jeopardy!* She submitted to this for a while, but the novelty of hearing her parents bellow *"What is postmodernism?"* or *"What is a subduction zone?"* over each other quickly faded. Although she'd usually stay in the room because it was the only television I allowed during the week—and she'd take those sweet, radiant phosphors any way she could get them—it didn't mean she was having fun. But one night in late April, as I was heading toward the kitchen to start dinner, I heard Alice chirp, "Who was Charles Guiteau?"

A moment later, after *none* of the contestants buzzed in, Alex Trebek's plummy voice echoed: "Who was Charles Guiteau?" As Alice clicked her tongue in mock disgust at anyone who didn't know who shot President Garfield, I stopped in my tracks, turned and stared at the back of her head. I had no recollection of ever discussing James A. Garfield's assassination with her.

"How did you know that?"

"Assassins," she explained, without looking away from the television.

Oh. Right. A few months earlier, thanks to her father, Alice had developed a fondness for the music of *West Side Story*, which led to other Stephen Sondheim musicals like *Sweeney Todd*, *Into the Woods* and, eventually, *Assassins*—a bouncy little soufflé about people who long to kill American presidents. For my part, I was so happy she hadn't taken a liking to "Send in the Clowns" that I never stopped to consider she might learn something from show tunes, especially *obscure* show tunes. Still, there it was. Charles Guiteau had, indeed, assassinated James A. Garfield. If we had not homeschooled this year, would Alice have found the time or inclination to develop a passion for Stephen Sondheim? If she learned about the tragic history of American political bloodshed from a Broadway musical instead of a history text, was that bad? If we continued to homeschool, would she continue to discover the world in her own unique way? Or would she merely end up owning the world's largest memorabilia collection from dinner-theater productions of *Company*?

By late spring, my waffling was beginning to annoy everyone, especially me. But still, I could not pull the trigger. I could not decide whether to homeschool my daughter the following year. I needed a sign. I needed someone to show me that it would be okay. Okay to stay or okay to leave. I needed one more tribal expedition.

Melissa and I know each other in the modern way, which is to say we have an online friend in common and follow each other's blogs. The homeschooling mother of a large family, Melissa is a devout Catholic and a successful writer. She raises her six children. She travels. She wears something besides yoga pants. She has loyal readers, an aura of genuine serenity and enviable hair. Reading her blog, I learned that she's taught a Shakespeare class to her homeschool group for the past five years, and every year her students perform selected scenes from the play they've studied. This year's production, *Twelfth Night*, would be staged in a friend's backyard in two weeks. Shamelessly, I invited myself to the show.

My first thought upon entering the gate was, "Alice must never know we could be living like this." The yard was huge and filled with things to climb and swing on. There were approximately fifty people in attendance, about half of whom were parents or visiting adults. This group all identified themselves as very observant Catholic homeschoolers. A few were unschoolers, but there was no evidence of the gentle anarchy I had come to expect from my first exposure, which is to say not one of these children removed his or her pants. I was pleased, however, to notice what I've come to think of as the traditional unschooling indicator: chickens, pecking away in a coop near the garage.

A rope had been stretched between two trees with a couple of sheets hanging down from either side. The cast huddled behind the sheets. The audience sat in folding chairs out front, except for those who chose to observe from a nearby tree house. The smallest family had four children; the largest had nine. There were far more children than roles to play, so the parts were rotated among all the actors, who ranged in age from five to sixteen. The smallest players stood up very tall and straight; many of them shouted their lines quite clearly. All three Violas were lovely to watch. One of the more popular Sir Toby Belches did, in fact, belch. While every child may not have grasped the meaning behind every line, they were all quite comfortable with Shakespeare's language and cadences. They understood the story well enough to convey it to the audience. They understood the humor well enough to sell the jokes. I've seen far worse productions starring professional actors.

At intermission, some of us stretched our legs by walking over to inspect the chickens. This created such a spirit of bonhomie among the audience that I found myself thinking theaters should consider replacing popcorn with fresh eggs.

The second act was mercifully abridged. As the final curtain dropped—or more accurately, slid—the audience applauded loudly and everyone wandered back to the house to enjoy *Twelfth Night*–themed snacks including boot-shaped cookies iced with yellow garters (act 2, scene 5) and thick potato chips laced with vinegar and pepper (act 3, scene 4). There were also lots of sandwiches, fruit trays and juice boxes; these might not have been Shakespearean exactly, but while music might be the food of love (act 1, scene 1), the food of children comes in bulk. The victuals were eaten and the children tumbled back outside to climb, run, shout and generally pursue blissful exhaustion on their own terms.

I sat on the deck and watched the happy chaos around me. Technically, this wasn't my tribe. The house was filled with Catholic iconography. These were families who arrange their lives around the liturgical season. But the group welcomed me graciously, and I basked in the afternoon light and the many things we agreed on. These families believed learning Shakespeare was important, but so was running around with your friends on a glorious spring day. I believed this, also. They believed in placing the Catholic faith at the center of their lives. I didn't. They believed homeschooling was worth the time and effort. With reservations, so did I. They believed in the benefits of raising poultry. Me, too. (We'll convert Daniel, eventually.) Maybe the lesson here is that we don't have to share 84.7 percent of our basic beliefs to belong to a tribe. The fact was, Alice would have had a wonderful time in that yard that afternoon. Maybe we just have to agree that our children deserve the best start we can give them—without having to agree on a precise definition of what "best start" actually means.

* * *

The twentieth century brought more changes in each of its decades than had been seen in any previous century. Daniel's father clearly remembered when people in his neighborhood still used horses for transportation—his neighborhood in New York City. For his eighty-seventh birthday, Poppop bought himself an iPad. The twenty-first century will throw changes our way at an even more accelerated rate. Everyone knows this—it's been a talking point for at least twenty years—but we still don't seem to get it. As parents, and as teachers, we concern ourselves with bromides like *critical thinking* and *reform*, but as each year comes and goes, the education we're promising our children continues to devolve into a two-ingredient concoction: one part guess and one part hope. Cross your fingers, kids.

There's a concept in anthropology called the "liminal state." The liminal state is the state between states. It's a threshold, a moment of uncertainty when things are being broken down and reformed, when central values are questioned and reshaped. The anthropologist Victor Turner wrote that during this state "the very structure of society [is] temporarily suspended . . ." Being caught in a liminal state can be raw and disorienting but it can also open up one's thinking to new possibilities, and this holds true for an individual or an entire culture experiencing its effects.

Right now, the institutions of American education—Big Ed—are in a liminal state. What worked once obviously doesn't work anymore, but what comes next is still unclear. As a rule, human beings hate the liminal state, sensing it to be a dangerous, uncertain condition to be avoided whenever possible. This is why we tend to build rituals around periods of change. Baptisms, weddings and funerals all share a liminal characteristic. Whether it's unschooling, Tiger Mom-ing, using Wisdom Books or raiding the retirement fund to pay for an academically rigorous preschool, parents often decide the way they've chosen to educate their children is the best choice, the only logical choice, because that feels better than the truth, which is we have no idea what's going to work. Not a clue.

Faced with a very foggy road ahead of us, we are probably best served by understanding there is just so much we can predict, and so much we can't. We need to acknowledge that we're all trying our best—homeschoolers and brick-and-mortar schoolers alike. After that, we need to embrace the uncertainty and just hope everything turns out better than bad.

I thanked my hostess profusely and grabbed my purse. I glanced back at the lively yard and thought, *Maybe I can bring the kid back for next year's show.* I got in the car and turned off the radio. I needed to have a nice long think.

Graduation

* * *

When I was a girl, I had a habit of lolling around the house being listless in an especially obvious manner. My mother would eventually ask what I was doing. "Nothing." I'd sigh droopily. To which she'd respond, "How will you know when you're done?"

If you homeschool, you will spend a good chunk of any given day helping your child factor a polynomial, frame a discussion, fold origami, undangle a participle, field a baseball, conjugate a verb, find Zimbabwe on a map, fire up a browser, figure out the periodic table and do whatever else is required to answer a thousand questions and solve a thousand problems. But there's one question many parents aren't prepared for: How do you know when you're done?

What does the finish line look like?

Over the years, homeschoolers have adapted a number of the more traditional rites of passage to fit their unique requirements. There was one particular ritual I wanted to experience up close and I was running late. The driver ahead of me might have been suffering from severe tachophobia or been under the delusion that driving the speed limit would cause a tear in the space-time continuum. No problem, I thought. They never start these things on time. The ceremony was scheduled to begin at two. Alice and I loped into the hotel ballroom at precisely four minutes past. The participants were already onstage. The main speaker was already speaking. A few members of the audience shot me that sideways look you hit people with when they arrive late. I cringed apologetically and noticed that one of the glaring guests was wearing a three-piece suit made entirely from tie-dyed denim. A few women quietly nursed their babies. Small boys raced in and out of the ballroom playing tag. A man sitting on the inside aisle wore a T-shirt that advised: *Don't ask me about my dissertation*. On his back was a pair of feathery angel wings. Not a silk-screened image of wings. Actual wings.

Yes, my daughter and I had just crashed a homeschool graduation ceremony.

There were nine graduates onstage, each wearing a customized version of a cap and gown, some more customized than others. The commencement speaker was a professional storyteller, an avuncular fellow who records his own versions of classic American tales on CD for families to listen to at home. If you ever find yourself in the position of having to recruit a commencement speaker, I strongly suggest you look into a professional storyteller. The "storyteller" will know how to keep your audience entertained and engaged; the "professional" will understand that time equals money. This particular storyteller was motivating, illuminating and brief.

"A life can be well lived," he began, "if you find someone who really loves you for who you are; if you find something you love to do and you find someplace that feels like home." His advice for those going to college was the same as it was for the teens going straight to work. Start with the things that interest you. When you get out in the real world, don't forsake your curiosity, your willingness to think differently from those around you, your eagerness to try new things. The storyteller recalled Will Rogers's observation that we are all ignorant on many different subjects. When you find the thing you're gifted at—and you will if you look for it—accomplishment may seem easy. Never take your natural gifts for granted; share them with your community in joy and confidence. But never forget that each and every one of us is ignorant about something, and take joy in that, also.

I'm not a Will Rogers scholar, but it all sounded plausible and certainly apropos for a high school commencement. In fact, the whole speech was quite moving and remarkably free of graduation clichés; the speaker never once referred to stairways to the future, pathways to the future, bridges to the future or any other chewed-over architectural metaphor. At the end, he wished everyone luck and walked offstage. I checked my watch: fifteen minutes. I've attended graduation ceremonies where the invocation delivered by the assistant secretary to the vice principal lasted longer than that. I've never felt more fondness toward the entire homeschool community.

The host for the evening rose to the podium to explain that the parents would be invited onstage to give each of the graduates their diplomas because, after all, the parents were the educators.

The first graduate was an opera singer whose original music had been performed by his local orchestra. He approached the microphone tentatively. "Feels like yesterday I was playing *Counter-Strike* six hours a night," he told the crowd, proving that even opera singers/composers are still teenage boys. He blinked back tears, held up his diploma and softly said, "Whoo!"

The second boy's mother was crying before she reached the stage. "He's overcome so many obstacles," she sniffled proudly. "Being diagnosed with Type One diabetes when he was eight, he stayed strong even when I fell apart. He's always been our rock. He will stick to it." His six-year-old brother, invited to speak, stood on tiptoes to reach the microphone and barked, "Chris, you're graduating, bye." Everyone laughed.

Chris accepted his diploma from his family with a few mumbled thanks and then fell silent, wiping away his own tears. His little brother piped up, "This is why we told you to practice your speech." He was off-mic this time, but everyone heard it and laughed again.

One mother commended her daughter for always knowing when and how to ask for help. The mother quoted Albus Dumbledore: "It is our choices, Harry, that show what we truly are, far more than our abilities." The daughter picked her mother up and swung her around in glee. Everyone laughed.

A single mother in a tie-dyed shirt thanked family, friends, God and her country for granting her the freedom to educate her children as she chose. Her daughter looked out at the audience, smiled shyly and said, "When people asked my mom what she was teaching me, she always said, 'We're doing . . . stuff.' Well, I'm very grateful for the opportunity to have done stuff."

One father listed all of his daughter's accomplishments. All of them. We listened politely. His daughter had accomplished a great deal and he was justifiably proud of her. Still, as the encomium wore on, some of us may have been praying that the parents who came next would have a little less to crow about. The man ended his paean with the declaration, "Homeschool will bring America back to its roots: hardworking, imaginative citizens!" This elicited a spontaneous and enthusiastic cheer, possibly out of passionate agreement, possibly out of gratitude the speech was over.

The next father discussed his prerequisites for allowing his daughter to graduate. She must demonstrate that she can educate herself; she had proved this to him. She must seek a vocation that sparks her passion and demands the discipline to master it; she had done that. For the third requirement, he turned to the audience and asked: "She has to be a good friend, a true friend. So, do you want her as a best friend?"

Her friends in the audience applauded and hooted. Everyone else joined in. The beaming father handed his daughter her diploma and they fell into each other's arms.

The next mother said through tears, "We've loved each other, we've been kind to each other . . ." She couldn't go on, so her husband took over. Voice wobbling, he said, "It's the fingerprints you put on a story that make it special. Perfectionism is boring. I look forward to see what fingerprints you leave on this world."

The girl took her diploma and said, "I can't thank my parents enough for what they've done for me." At which point she joined everyone onstage for a family cry.

The last boy's father was deployed in Afghanistan, but his mother and grandparents joined him triumphantly onstage. His mother called him "a compassionate young man, the most wonderful person I know." His grandfather said, "He's a good boy, can strip an engine in half a day. He has good hands and a very good mind." The boy took his mother's hand, and his grandmother's, and spoke clearly. "We're not done, ever. We learn until we can't learn anymore. I want to thank my family for helping me to learn, forcing me to learn. I will do this forever."

The host gathered the graduates for a standing ovation. Laudatory music came over the sound system as the kids beamed and everyone snapped pictures. After about a minute, the music cut out suddenly. People laughed. And then we trooped into the hallway for cake.

Getting back on the freeway I thought: Did this work? Did this experiment in homeschooling benefit these people? Taking the long view, it's way too soon to tell. Let's check in again when they're thirty, or fifty, or being eulogized by their grandchildren. More immediately, two of these children were going to a four-year college in September, four were going to community college and three were off to have adventures. Considering that California is currently amputating community college programs for financial reasons, and tuitions even at state colleges are soaring beyond the reach of many families, the obstacles to completing an undergraduate degree were formidable. But that was true for anyone graduating from high school nowadays.

What sweetened the odds for the graduates I'd seen today, it seemed to me, were factors no policy wonk could measure. Each of these children had a family who knew them intimately and loved who they had become. Every one of these teenagers was passionately interested in something and seemed eager to pursue it. Recently, I had attended a private school commencement where several hundred identically robed kids had massed on a football field, shuffled to a podium and tossed their caps in unison after the diplomas were distributed. Virtually all the students were headed straight to college—mostly to the kind of institutions parents bumper-sticker their car with. On the surface, those children would seem to be starting off at least one lap ahead of the homeschoolers. But the graduates I'd seen today seemed more confident, more focused and more active participants in their own education than the prep school grads. I wouldn't place any bets on which group will find more success or fulfillment as adults.

Driving home, we fell into the semi-somnambulant rhythm of freeway travel. Alice flipped though a book in the backseat while I drifted in and out of a dozen internal conversations. I imagined myself at Alice's graduation, whatever that turned out to be. I imagined what I might say and what she might say as we handed her the diploma. I imagined restricting Daniel's comments to one minute—two minutes, tops—and insisting that everyone rehearse beforehand. Alternately, I saw Daniel and me sitting among hundreds of families, watching Alice walk across the stage, getting her diploma from her principal. Either way, I saw my daughter smiling.

I imagined coming to the end of her high school years and asking myself the most important question, the question whose answer would tell us whether we'd given Alice the best education we could. But what was this question? I knew it wasn't the one I'd asked in the laundry room: "Will this break the child?" Later, I'd thought the question was: "Did I get her everything she needed, academically?" But that wasn't quite it, either.

After watching these families for an afternoon—for a year—I had come to realize the only question worth asking before I sent Alice off into the world would be: "Have I given you the strength to take the baton from here?" Strength is the love you give them, and the faith (of whatever orthodoxy, or lack thereof) that guides them. Strength is the things you teach them, and the times you step back and let them figure things out for themselves. Regarding my daughter, my definition of strength includes: resiliency, a sense of humor, the resolve to work hard on something you don't like (especially when the Internet is bursting with pictures of cats) and being able to do your own laundry.

As we turned onto our street, I saw a vision of Alice in her cap and gown, Daniel and me embracing her. At the end of this experiment we call Alice's childhood, I imagine if she's as eager to move ahead with her passions as the graduates I'd just met, and as fond of her family as these kids seemed to be of theirs, I'll have my answer.

Parent/Teacher Conference

* * *

It's now the end of August. Alice is sitting at her laptop in the kitchen. Daniel and I hover nearby, knocking back the first caffeine of the morning and staying out of camera range. Alice is wearing a headset, listening to distant voices. On a practical level, she's attending an online orientation meeting. On a metaphorical level, she's moving into a new world.

Last spring, friends, relatives and chance acquaintances began asking us the same question over and over: Are you going to continue to homeschool your daughter? In the extended dance remix, this question became: *Are you going to continue to give Alice the benefits of one-on-one attention and open-ended time for self-discovery, to the possible detriment of her later ability to work in groups? Or are you going to send her back to a public/private school and take the chance she'll never develop a self-generated work ethic, but at least she'll get some time away from your weirdness?* Of course, what some of them really wanted to know was: *Quinn, will you ever wear real pants before noon again?*

I'd been asking myself the same questions. The answer to all of them turns out to be: maybe.

By the start of summer vacation, I had come to the conclusion that while homeschooling was turning out to be a pretty good fit for our family, I wanted Alice's education to be more than a three-person play. Daniel and I had done better as teachers than either of us might have expected, but I also wanted other, more experienced and specialized educators teaching her. So far, our homeschool experiment had produced a happy and balanced family dynamic; I wasn't eager to exchange that for a potentially hostile and corrosive middle school experience. On the other hand, I was acutely aware that my child's education was going to be a long and complex voyage, and after only one year at the helm I already knew I was running out of charts.

In fact, we'd decided to try a new approach to homeschooling: a live, online classroom taught by credentialed teachers. A little research turned up a handful of attractive offerings for middle schoolers, and one in particular appealed to Daniel and me. It was geared toward students like Alice, kids who were accelerated in one subject or another. Class time was used primarily for group discussion, and students were expected to take responsibility for their own course work. This sounded like the best of both worlds. Alice would have access to enthusiastic, scholarly teachers, yet she could still be working from home where Daniel and I could help as needed or—in my case—possibly learn a thing or two. The classes would be live, interactive sessions with children from ten different time zones, so we did have to adhere to their schedule—but we would make up for this constraint by measuring our commute in yards and seconds instead of miles and hours. Classes were typically done by noon so we could continue our hikes and I still could drone on about the Sherman Antitrust Act should the opportunity present itself. I was pretty excited about that; Alice kept her feelings to herself.

The admissions process was daunting. By the time we gathered all the necessary forms, references, transcripts and other paperwork, the entire document was slightly thicker than my mortgage application had been. Among other things, Alice had six essay questions to answer, while we, her parents, had two. I declared essay writing to be an educational priority and arranged her schedule for an entire month around creating and refining these compositions. My poor child endured many eardrum-bleedingly boring lectures on how this was a valuable lesson in managing a big project by breaking it down into manageable tasks and setting aside enough time to do it well. I also took the opportunity to introduce key concepts regarding nonfiction prose, chestnuts like, *There is no writing, there is only rewriting*, and, *When in doubt, cut it out*. I droned on about the dangers of procrastination. Needless to say, I procrastinated writing the parent's essays until the night before the deadline and palmed them off onto Daniel at the very last minute, confirming yet again that Alice wasn't the only one who needed to learn a few things.

Six weeks later, we received word that Alice had been accepted for the fall session. Half of her classes would be self-directed, meaning she'd be working at home at her own speed; the other half would meet in a virtual classroom on a regular schedule.

This morning, Daniel and I watch Alice get used to her new classroom. Her computer screen features a virtual whiteboard with a frame down the left side listing the dozen or so students currently in attendance. Above the list is a live video of the instructor, a smiling woman in her thirties who seems to be working something out on her desk, just below the frame. Tucked smartly around the whiteboard are icons, buttons, boxes, toolbars and widgets indicating a menu of nifty functions such as *Raise Hand*, *Draw*, *Clap*, *Laugh*, and *Step Out*. The entire setup resembles one of those futuristic telecom commercials that promise all sorts of miraculous 9G features, but which actually suck once you've signed a two-year contract. This program, however, seems to be working. At the designated start time, the teacher activates her microphone and announces apologetically that she needs another minute or two to upload some files to the whiteboard. Meanwhile, she says, the students can communicate with one another using the text-chat function on the lower left of the screen. In less than a second, words and sentences began popping up in the box:

Where are you?

How old are you?

Do you have pets? What do you like to read?

They are ten, eleven and twelve years old. They live in Oregon, Alaska, California, Texas, New York, Hong Kong and Denmark.

One student is stationed temporarily in Romania while her mother finishes a job. Some of them are enrolled in this program part-time while also attending a regular school, some are part-time because the rest of their education is traditional homeschooling. Nearly all of them have read *The Lord of the Rings*. Several have cats or dogs—Alice being one of two with a cat sitting in her lap as she types. The children are still eagerly getting acquainted when the teacher switches off the chat window. It is time for class to begin.

When I was a kid, the year 2000 was shorthand for The Future, which we understood to mean jet packs and Thanksgiving dinner in a pill. We got the specifics wrong but the generalities right. Alice was born in the year 2000. She has never used a record player or dialed a rotary phone. Her first correspondence to a pen pal was by email. She is the only one of her peers to live without a cell phone—a fact she notes with melodramatic frequency. In the developed world, people under twenty-five don't view the computer as a privilege or a novelty but as a vital organ. We are online today because that's where life is.

This circles back to the question of whether Alice will continue homeschooling forever or return eventually to what many friends refer to as "real school." It's a reasonable question, especially as parents today feel as though they have one option or the other, and the stakes are high either way. For our family, this no longer seems like a binary decision—and I think for most Americans, the choice will start to become less *either/or* and more *how much of each*.

Recently, I saw an ad for a popular online dating site that proclaims one in five couples today meet online. These couples, should they get married and get busy, probably won't be surprised if their children's best educational options are available via webcam. Parents whose earliest memories include Baby Einstein tapes or who buy computer games for their three-year-old offspring aren't going to be as squeamish as an earlier generation might have been about online education. But for most families, online classes might be only part of the curriculum. It won't be homeschooling as we've known it, but it won't be brick-and-mortar schooling, either. This is a society very pleased with the idea of watching what they watch on their schedule, not the television station's schedule, and buying exactly what songs they like and not paying for the whole CD including the ten-minute vanity drum solo. It's all about choices. In the iTunes version of institutional learning, meaningful lessons can originate from the large redbrick building down the street, from a recreation center downtown, from a music studio in Seattle or a lecture hall in London. Over the next decade, I think homeschooling will become *roam* schooling. And I think it's already happening.

In the two years before we started doing it, I thought about homeschooling. Not often, but sometimes, especially during those quiet moments when I was emptying her backpack and I'd find English assignments I knew she could do in her sleep or the dreaded long division she'd bat around like a cat toy from semester to semester. I'd chew on the inside of my mouth and think, *I could never homeschool*, and then I'd wander off to find the workbooks I had gotten for Alice to strengthen her math or encourage her writing. Looking back, it turns out I *was* homeschooling; I was just doing it part-time. If you're the parent of a school-aged child, I submit you're probably doing it to some extent as well.

We are far more involved with homework than most of our parents ever were, not to mention music lessons and sports practices and cultural activities that occur well beyond the aegis of a school district. And what about the unique needs of individual students? If your child is outside the norm in any way, you're probably using independent resources to help him catch up or finding extra ways to challenge him. You're likely also paying extra, in the form of extra fees or "voluntary donations," for anything beyond the three Rs and PE. If not, good for you—but don't be shocked if things turn sour in a hurry.

It's been an interesting few years here in my home state, especially if you're a fan of financial catastrophes. If California were a person, he'd have maxed out every one of his credit cards, watched the repo guy take his car and moved onto a friend's couch. Considering the last grizzly bear in California died in the 1920s, we should change the official state animal to the canary in the coalmine. When the current global financial tsunami rolled in (to switch metaphors yet again), we were hit early and hard—and we responded by slashing school funding. Sixty percent of California's budget cuts have come from public education. We're the most populous state in the union and rank forty-sixth in per-student spending. I'll let the economists ponder the deeper significance of that spread, but I can tell you what it looks like on the ground. Neighbors and friends who can't afford private school are volunteering as fund-raisers, janitors, art teachers, orchestra leaders, coaches and classroom assistants for their children's public or charter schools. Sound familiar? At what point does every home in the neighborhood participate somehow in the local public school? At what point does the public school up the street contribute part of a neighborhood's homeschooling syllabus? If these trends are allowed to evolve naturally, roam schooling won't be a jet-pack fantasy. It will be a practical solution.

The annual growth rate for homeschooling is about 7 percent. I like to use that figure because it's the lowest number I could find. That's a lot of families convinced their local schools don't work. Sure, many of those parents are homeschooling because of religious beliefs, and some are steadfastly off the grid and would never be part of traditional education, but a growing number of homeschoolers are just like my family. They started out in a brick-and-mortar school but decided it didn't suit their child's needs. And as public school budgets shrivel and private school tuitions explode, the ranks of ordinary, nonsectarian homeschoolers may eventually outgrow those other cohorts.

Thanks to online search tools, families can shop a vast global marketplace for products they want at prices they're willing to pay. Nobody expects all young people to enjoy the same twenty or thirty songs; why should they be limited to the same dozen or so classes? Again, the iTunes model is a useful reference for the future of education. If you're thinking something like, *Public education will never change, it's too big!* I'd respectfully point out that the music business looked like an invincible Goliath before digital technology raised its slingshot. Many experts assumed the all-powerful music industry would survive the emergence of file sharing, but music fans were intrigued by nimble and consumer-friendly alternatives to Big Music. In less than a decade, a multibillion-dollar industry collapsed under its own weight and its own misguided attempts at self-preservation. Once the meteor hit the planet, there was no way to set things back to "normal." If you were a dinosaur, it was all over.

The vast institutional dominance wielded by Big Ed's major players—politicians, bureaucrats and unions—will succumb to the inevitable glow in the sky. The meteor is on its way, pulled by the gravitational force of a million disgruntled parents. Will the dinosaur suffer as its organs fail? Probably. But the dinosaur is not our concern. Our children are our concern.

Today, the American educational system is huge, with nearly fifty-four million students, K through 12. Nothing personal, but when it comes to decision-making, any one single kid isn't a compelling concern to the system. Neither is the single teacher who used to love her job but now struggles with having to foist a standardized test on a classroom with twice as many students as five years ago; or the single administrator who spends every day trying to stretch a shrinking budget over increasing demands. For change to occur, it's going to take an army of parents who don't want to abandon the promise of public education but are prepared to answer the hardest question of all: "Why can't public schools be better than this?"

Today, the average American family can access more information than the combined libraries of Harvard, Oxford and the Sorbonne only one generation ago. The Department of Labor predicts that today's learner will have ten different occupations by the age of forty-two. We can't even *conceive* of the jobs our children will be vying for in the next decade. Some economists have suggested a gold watch for a lifetime of service will be as rare fifteen years from now as a homeschooler was fifteen years ago. To succeed in the new century, American education is going to have to become smaller and more nimble, taking what resources it needs from anywhere it can get it.

Imagine your high school junior spends half of every day at the brick-and-mortar school up the street. Two afternoons a week, he logs into an art history seminar being taught by a grad student in Paris. He takes a computer animation class at the local community college. He sings in the church choir and dives at the community pool. He studies web design on YouTube and debate on Facebook. He and three classmates see a tutor from the community college who preps them for AP Chemistry. He studies Spanish online whenever he wants, takes cooking lessons at a local restaurant every Saturday morning and chats with his guidance counselor every other day on Skype. Is he homeschooling? Is he regular schooling? Who cares, he's learning. More important, as with the songs in his personal playlist, you've assembled a curriculum that works for him. It's *his* education. I suspect he's more likely to have a real education, an education that sticks, if he's part of shaping it.

Then again, I could be completely wrong about all of this.

I do know that I'm not as miserable and fearful as I was the second day of this adventure but I imagine people walking up the steps to the hangman's scaffold were less miserable and fearful than I was that day. I'm still nowhere near as confident about homeschooling as some of the parents I've met this year and I probably never will be. This education we're giving Alice is an experiment and not every experiment succeeds. But after nearly a year of doing this, I feel considerably better about the choices we're making. Alice will learn and she will blossom and she will have friends. If her current education stops working, I hope I will have the clarity to figure out what she needs and the fortitude to get it. I'm pretty certain the options will grow wider and more interesting with each passing year.

I also know that some lessons are best learned at a kitchen table and some lessons are best learned in a gymnasium, a lecture hall or a chemistry lab. It would be nice if every student had better access to every option, and I anticipate that over the next decade they will. The divisions between homeschooling and institutional schooling will continue to dissolve. We will go to the education and the education will come to us. The bad news: It doesn't work that way yet. The good news: We get to build it. For the first time in recent memory I'm looking at something that matters very, very much to me and feeling neither dread nor angst. Oddly enough, I'm feeling optimistic.

It's been an instructive year.

Alice is still online but she is now in her language orientation session. Her earphones are plugged in so Daniel and I can't hear it, but the teacher must be giving the students a little taste of what to expect. Alice is leaning forward, saying "hello" in Chinese, over and over again. "*Ni hao,*" she says, first tentatively and then with greater certainty, greeting her classmates, her school and her world, wherever that turns out to be.

Acknowledgments

Thanks to Marian Lizzi, who edits like a dream and stopped me from many of my worst impulses; I'm trying to arrange to have her edit my life. Kate Garrick is the agent I always wished I had and twice the agent I ever was. Gratitude to Melissa Broder and her glorious ability to make other people get excited about this book. Heartfelt thanks to Lauren Becker, who learned that I respond to nagging, eventually, and never called me a lazy fathead. Lisa Amoroso and Sara Wood, the cover art you created for the book delights me every time I look at it, and there aren't many things in this world that do that to me. To the Foley family, for being the first family who showed me that homeschoolers can look like me, only saner. To Michele East, Rachel Robinson and Victoria Stafford, for their friendship and their Alice-tending; may anyone reading this have such allies. Bobby Oswinski, who was supportive and excited about the book even when I wasn't. Raphael Simon, who first told me to write it. Allison Wright, for making sure my history facts were, in fact, facts; anything I got wrong, blame me. Nichole Torbitsky, for helping me parse the differences between Evangelists and Fundamentalists. Judy Haskell, Melodee Helms and John Rinciari, for keeping me honest. Ariel Carpenter and Arlene Wszalek, for their wise counsel. Stephanie Frizzell, Rose Dessaint and Louna Dessaint, for being lovely people and excellent educators. Melissa Wiley, for allowing me to intrude in her life. Howard Brock and Clyde Smith, thank you for making me look like me, only not tired or panicked. All the wonderful people I interviewed for the book who didn't make it into the book; I wish everyone had gotten to know how interesting you were. Ken Miller, who took on the Herculean task of finding the book in my writing and always saw what it could be, frequently when I didn't. I shudder to think of what it would have been like without him. And finally, to D. Because I'll never stop thanking him.

Further Reading

This isn't a complete list of the books I read while researching and writing this book, but each one of these titles illuminated and educated me in some way. If you're interested in learning more about homeschooling, they're a good place to start.

Unschooling Rules: 55 Ways to Unlearn What We Know About Schools and Rediscover Education by Clark Aldrich (Greenleaf Book Group, 2011)

A Little Way of Homeschooling by Suzie Andres (Hillside Education, 2011)

Homeschool: An American History by Milton Gaither (Palgrave Macmillan, 2008)

Highlighting Homeschooling: Empowering Parents and Inspiring Children by Dr. Bethany Gardiner (Sticky Tape Press, 2011)

Dumbing Us Down: The Hidden Curriculum of Compulsory Schooling by John Taylor Gatto (New Society Publishers, 2002)

The Underground History of American Education by John Taylor Gatto (Odysseus Group, 2000)

Weapons of Mass Instruction: A Schoolteacher's Journey Through the Dark World of Compulsory Schooling by John Taylor Gatto (New Society Publishers, 2010)

The Myths of Standardized Tests: Why They Don't Tell You What You Think They Do by Phillip Harris, Bruce M. Smith and Joan Harris (Rowman & Littlefield Publishers, 2011)

Teach Your Own: The John Holt Book of Home-schooling by John Holt and Patrick Farenga (Da Capo Press, 2003)

A Matter of Basic Principles by Don Veinot, Joy Veinot and Ron Henzel (Midwest Christian Outreach, 2003)

The Well-Trained Mind: A Guide to Classical Education at Home by Susan Wise Bauer and Jesse Wise (W. W. Norton & Company, 2009)

About the Author

Quinn Cummings is known to some as "the kid from that movie *The Goodbye Girl*," and others know her as "the kid from that show *Family*," while a few know her as the writer of *The QC Report*, a blog in which she has scrupulously recorded her failings and love of toast since 2005. Her work has appeared in publications including *Good Housekeeping*, *Newsweek* and many, many bake-sale flyers. She and her family live in Los Angeles, where she continues to homeschool her daughter. In her darker moments, Quinn fears her grade school principal is right and this is all going on her permanent record. This is her second book.